SIMPLY
RAYMOND

SIMPLY RAYMOND

RECIPES FROM HOME

Raymond Blanc

PHOTOGRAPHY BY CHRIS TERRY

Dedication

While I was writing my little book, *Simply Raymond*, my mother passed away. This book is dedicated with the utmost love to Maman Blanc. My inspiration to become a chef, restaurateur and hotelier stems from my mother's desire and compulsion to give, share and, of course, to feed a family of seven. She was a muse to me, shaping my approach to food and people. Her values formed the foundations of my cooking and career. She has brought happiness to so many, in the kitchen and at the table. Maman, your life was long, your loss is great. Your legacy, however, is immense.

CONTENTS

Of the many cookery books that I have written, this one has the most extraordinary story.

When I embarked on a project to publish a collection of recipes, it should have led me along a familiar path. After all, I was not a newcomer to the business of creating cookbooks. Instead, with this one, I found myself on an especially strange journey. A journey with plenty of unknowns, and with some darkness. Yet here we are – the journey has ended at this very happy, bright destination, where you and I are united through food, the joy of cookery and the sheer pleasures of eating and sharing.

You will be eager to skip ahead and throw yourself into the cooking of the dishes. But, first, sit back please, and give me just a moment to tell you how it came about …

It was a couple of decades ago, or even longer, that I began to dream of writing a book that would specifically pay homage to two great inspirations. Both had been the mentors who inspired me to fully appreciate and relish simple cooking at its best.

One of these inspirational figures was my mother, who every day made lunch and dinner for her husband and their five children. Maman had a passion for pleasing people by feeding them. I felt encouraged, compelled to cook. Soon I was in love with it and, to this day, I am still at my happiest when feeding others, and teaching. (True, I now present a bill to the guests, while Maman never did such a thing, though she certainly should have – and could have – done.) My mother's values were ingrained in me – the foundations of a career, a life. Without such values, I could never have won the praise, the prizes and the plaudits that I have.

The other inspiration was someone I never met. Edouard de Pomiane was a Frenchman, scientist and author. He was also a connoisseur who wrote so well about food and, as a young man, I adored the witty, friendly, conversational style of his book, *La Cuisine en Dix Minutes* – or, in English, *Cooking in Ten Minutes*. The book was published in 1930, which shows how far ahead he was of his time.

Pomiane was quirky, confident and maybe a bit over the top (like me). I was in awe of his ability to demystify cooking and make food inclusive. With my nose buried in the pages of his best-selling book, I was transported to a gastronomic heaven of the finest home cooking.

Well, a multitude of ideas constantly whizzes around in my mind. And so it was a couple of decades ago, or even longer, that these were now joined by another: it was the idea for that book of no-nonsense recipes. These would include the sorts of things that Maman Blanc made in her kitchen in our home beside the forests of Franche-Comté.

Chez Blanc, she had no brigades of chefs, fancy gadgets and high-tech equipment, such as a sous-vide machine, which people like me take for granted. She did not depend on the bleep-bleep of a food probe, or the ring-a-ting-ting of a timer. Maman relied on her senses as a guide, although she had an electric hand whisk and a cocotte minute, the French pressure cooker loved by a nation's mamans, and it had a useful timer. I implore all cooks to use their senses more often. Taste, taste, taste and let it guide you to the finish. Listen out for the difference in culinary sounds, be it the gentlest simmer or the rapid, rolling boil. When you are at the hob, listen for the noises of bubble, sizzle, the hiss and the spit. From the pan and pot, the tray or the roasting tin, food talks to the cook.

> ## I really do hope that soon these recipes will be a part of your repertoire and, as a result, that you will have requests for this or that.

Meanwhile, in my head, I could hear Pomiane's chatty, enthusiastic tone. I thought it would be the perfect pairing for the rustic food that my mother cooked, and so many others – me included – like to make. That way, I felt, I would have paid tribute to these two people and their influence upon me.

Looking back on my notes, I am reminded that I told myself this was to be a book 'to cherish and treasure', celebrating 'family and warmth'. Back then, I dreamt that it would become what it has indeed become now – an essential guide for you, the cook at home, filled with uncomplicated recipes for wholesome, delicious dishes, many of them French, some British, and others inspired by my travels. I really do hope that soon they will be a part of your repertoire and, as a result, that you will have requests for this or that.

This book was just an idea, a hope, a wish, a dream. The seasons came and went, and came and went again, and the years rolled by. The idea stayed with me, a recurring thought. Then one day, early in 2020, I was invited to the offices of Headline Publishing, beside the Thames, once a river rich in oysters. And the world of cookery is your oyster. Learn how to make one soup, and you can make hundreds. Master the art of pan-frying, and you can cook thousands of dishes, with no problems at all. Look at me – I was not born a baby cook. I had to learn, just like you and everyone else. Although mostly I learnt from my gifted mum, with her *paysan* approach, her values and her natural respect for seasonality, which inspired the naming of Le Manoir aux Quat'Saisons.

Excitedly, I spoke with the publishers, Lindsey and Kate, recounting my vision for the book. I told them about my beloved Maman, and of Pomiane's influence on my life. 'This book,' I said, 'will be a tribute to my mum and to a man I have never met, a man who way back could see the future of food …'

We talked about dishes that would be extremely quick to make, and wanted most of them to take within ten minutes or a little bit longer. As an affectionate tribute to my hero, Pomiane, this book would take a similar title to his own, *Cooking in Ten Minutes … or a Little Bit Longer*. We said farewell, shook hands and, as you can imagine, French-style, we kissed each other on both cheeks. Little did we know that within weeks these age-old social customs would be forbidden and regarded as frightening.

Woodcuts after Toulouse Lautrec

Cooking in – 10 Minutes

Edouard de Pomiane
300 Recipes

CASSIRER

In March 2020, Great Britain went into lockdown. The world was about to change. The coronavirus pandemic was here. Convenience vanished. Shopping for food became difficult. The culture of the sandwich at the office desk was no more. The shops that made sandwiches were closed, and offices with the desks were shut. Most of us stayed at home, though millions continued as 'key workers', and to them, we shall always be indebted.

On my own, and in my flat in London, I would call my mum in France. A woman of less than five feet, she had never let her lack of height get in the way of a good meal. I think of her, a loveable, funny, little woman, quickly moving a chair from one cupboard to another in a frantic search for sugar, salt or a spice, and then she'd realise, 'Ah, it's on the table.'

And I found myself craving, and then cooking, childhood meals, simple to make and full of goodness. All of them could be rustled up speedily – tartiflette, a plate of crudités, a morteau sausage salad, an onion or tomato soup, and the one that my mother made with the season's vegetables and chervil. I was her young helper and runner. The family meals began with me being sent from the house to my father's cherished, well-nourished, immaculately kept potager to gather the ingredients. '*Mon petit*, go into the garden and get me …' (Mon petit is a phrase that I often call a lot of my chefs, especially when I cannot remember names.)

I realised that all of these dishes would have to be included in this book, and so they are, along with classics such as Caesar salad, salade Niçoise and a ratatouille (my version is quick to cook).

Since 1984, I have spent so much of my time in the kitchens at Le Manoir aux Quat'Saisons and Brasserie Blanc, but now my professional life was a struggle, filled with tremendous stress and strains; the turmoil of a business put on hold. You encountered hardship too, I am sure, whether it was personal or professional, or both. Slowly, however, I began to really relish the fun that comes from cooking at home. I took to social media, sharing recipes that my British friends would call 'easy-peasy'.

I started to wonder about the book, and how it might be affected by the way you and I were cooking. More importantly, I began to understand how this pandemic would impact on our lifestyles and the food we eat. We will seriously tackle food waste, and we will be closer to our farmers, butchers, fishmongers, cheesemakers and our other food producers. We need to reconnect more with seasonality and the provenance and authenticity of produce. Sustainability must be the driving force in the years to come, and we will rediscover our skills, grow more and import less: good for the farmers and the economy. By digging into the past, we shall find our future. (Maybe I am just an old romantic, but I do believe, truly from my heart of hearts, that this will happen.)

I found myself craving, and then cooking, childhood meals.

As the weeks of solitude progressed, it was as if we had been 'given' more time. We devoted this time to the garden (the weather was glorious), to yoga, puzzles, TV boxsets. And the cooks among us spent that extra time in the kitchen.

The fast, fast world in which we lived had stopped zooming along, and was now in slow motion. The hurried breakfast bowl of cornflakes made way for the deep, rich scents of freshly baked banana loaf. The cheap burger on the hop was replaced by the cheerful barbecue in the garden. People spoke of finding positives in this new climate of negatives and, for those of us who love to cook, we did not need to search too far for pleasure.

Cooking in Ten Minutes now seemed too restrictive, unsuited to this new world. We all need a little bit longer in the kitchen, I thought to myself. And often quite a bit longer. Time was no longer a crucial factor behind the recipes, yet the spirit of my little book remained the same: wonderful, inexpensive dishes to bring a smile to the cook as well as those who are around the table. I regard cooking as an art of giving, the most natural and most powerful way of bringing people together. It is not a race against the clock.

If this book were to be an honest tribute to my mother and Pomiane, as well as an accurate reflection of my beliefs, along with the fact that we were all wishing to value our time, then the title would need to change. Quite simply, it had to celebrate simplicity.

I had drawn up a list of a few hundred recipes and began to refine it, taking me closer to a hundred (though I don't like to be confined by the dreaded restrictions of maths). I wanted to share with you my recipes from my culture, as well as other cultures. I wanted to show you how, apart from French dishes, I like to make an easy risotto, dhal, samosas. I wanted recipes for one-pot dishes, as well as a few slow-cooked, rustic treats, which melt in the mouth. This is a book in which the recipes illustrate cooking techniques that open up numerous opportunities. Remember, a recipe is only a template, a map to take you on an adventure.

Then I added to the list – delicious desserts without any culinary challenges: stewed apricots with crunchy almonds, roasted peaches, tarte boulangère and a strawberry and mascarpone tart that guarantees a 'Wow'.

A few months into lockdown, I received the phone call that I had dreaded. Death is in all of our lives. None of us can escape it. My Maman had died. She had coronavirus, although it was not the disease that caused her death. Instead, she died after a fall while trying to get out of her bed. She could have called for help to leave the bed but did not want to disturb the nurses. At the age of 97, her final act was one of characteristic thoughtfulness.

I was desperately sad not to have been there at her side. She had been at mine throughout my life.

She was the daughter of a farmer. At the age of 14 she left school to help in the fields, and her broad, tough-skinned hands told a tale of hard, manual labour. And while Mum didn't learn much in the classroom, she made up for it in the kitchen. I can picture her at home, darting around the garden as she gathered vegetables and herbs for a fantastic soup, which she'd blend with her moulin-légumes, the classic French food mill.

I remember catching my first fish, a tench almost as big as me. I was so proud and thrilled that I kissed the fish on its lips. At home, Maman slow-roasted the tench in a silky sauce of butter and lemon.

I can see her, too, at the dining table at home, as we ate lapin à la moutarde, in which the rabbit is braised with white wine and mustard. Maman sat with a fork in hand, a smile on her lips, and tears on her cheeks. The smile because she loved the taste. The tears ran down her cheeks because she adored the rabbits that we kept. Such is the French paradox.

Lapin à la moutarde was among the main courses I cooked at my first restaurant, Les Quat'Saisons. Within these pages is a recipe for chicken in a mustard sauce. It is made like my mother's rabbit dish, but with her in mind, and for those who love rabbits, I have used *le poulet* as a substitute.

I remember Christmases, almost right up to my mother's final one, when she would phone in advance of my arrival: 'Raymond! Don't forget to bring the Christmas pudding …' I wouldn't have dreamt of such a thing! Although I must confess there were a few times when I almost left it on the luggage rack on Eurostar (like an edible Christmas gift for the next passenger to take my seat).

My mother lived her life in Franche-Comté. Since my late twenties, I have lived in Britain. We were separated geographically and went for months without seeing each other. However, there is rarely a meal when I do not think of her.

It all seemed to happen so fast. First, a cough, which was not bad enough to stop me working on my book. Within two days, however, I was exhausted and then I felt ice cold, shaking uncontrollably and with a high fever. The Covid-19 test came back positive. I was admitted to the Covid high-dependency unit at the John Radcliffe in Oxford. For the next month, I would remain at the hospital.

Through Merry Christmas and Happy New Year, I was one of the many people who were being treated and cared for by the exceptional staff of the NHS. I was in awe of their commitment, their passion and devotion, as they worked long days and nights, always supportive and caring. They included Maude who, knowing that I was a chef, cooked me some delicious pasta and tomato sauce. Another nurse, Sally, sang beautifully as she worked, and one day – with her mask on – treated me to her rendition of 'La Vie en Rose'.

May I share a secret? For 30 years or more I have tried to meditate, but without any success. Always a new dish, or garden or a new room would interfere with my efforts. But there in my hospital bed, surrounded by tubes and beeping monitors, and in the middle of the night, suddenly meditation became my salvation. It was as if I could wrap myself in a sealed bubble of silence, remove negative thoughts and focus on taking in as much oxygen as possible in a tight-fitting mask; it was so difficult to breathe. The consultant saw that my oxygen levels were increasing, and she was so happy. On the whiteboard above my bed, she wrote: 'Wahoo! You won.' In the coming days, I needed less and less oxygen. Then I started to walk, a few steps at a time.

What about the food? The soups were suitably thin and hot, and I particularly liked the tomato and celery soup. I could not resist the mashed potatoes, the béchamel and flaked fish. The bean stew was nice and the meatballs were big. Often, I don't have desserts, but here I adored the amazing custard, especially when served with plums. I liked the rice pudding and the sticky toffee pudding (and you might like my recipe on page 273).

But my saving grace was that Natalia, my companion of 18 years, came to the hospital, leaving wonderful food for me at reception. She prepared the most delicious chicken soup, and nutritious goodies such as hard-boiled eggs with a salad of Black Russian tomatoes, smoked salmon with rye bread, hazelnut chocolate and dark chocolate (100% cocoa solids). These supplements did so much for my recovery.

> # I was in awe of their commitment, their passion and devotion, as they worked long days and nights, always supportive and caring.

After four weeks, I returned home. Natalia – a nutrition teacher at the RB Cookery School – spoiled me some more with sumptuous breakfasts of baked tomatoes, scrambled eggs, toasted spelt bread and the finest coffee. Lunch and dinners became such important moments of the day. Natalia was force-feeding me with kindness and the most wholesome, nutritious food. I started to regain the weight I had lost. I'd had time to contemplate the fragility of life and see that I was so lucky. I am grateful to know that I will make a full recovery. Out of this bad experience, I will take all the positives and change certain aspects of my life.

So, as you see, it has been the most extraordinary journey, but we have made it, and here we are, at this happy destination, united by food and cooking. As usual, I have spoken for far too long. I shall leave you to cook, have fun and celebrate. *Bon appétit!*

BREAKFAST AND BRUNCH

'The first lesson I teach my
new chefs: always taste, taste
and taste again. That's how you
get to know food and cooking,
and learn to build flavours.'

Flourless Banana Crêpes

PREP 5 MINS / COOK 10 MINS

These are the easy, speedy pancakes. The bananas should be extremely ripe, with a beautiful skin that's butterscotch yellow and speckled brown. Ripe means flavour and extra sweetness (though before serving you can also add the finest dusting of icing sugar, trickle of honey or maple syrup). Crêpes come with unhealthy connotations, but these ones cut out the culprits and have many health benefits. The eggs provide an extremely high protein content, and are also equipped with nearly every nutrient you need, including the more recently discovered essential nutrient, choline. Bananas, meanwhile, are rich in potassium, which helps to maintain a healthy heart and control blood pressure, and provide lots of vitamin C and B6, which support the immune system and nervous system respectively.

SERVES 4

2 large ripe bananas
4 medium eggs
  (preferably organic or
  free-range)
generous pinch of salt
2 tablespoons sunflower
  oil (or any other
  vegetable oil, rapeseed
  oil or 2 tablespoons
  unsalted butter)

To finish
fresh berries and 1 lemon,
  for squeezing, plus a
  choice of honey, maple
  syrup or icing sugar

With the back of a fork, mash the bananas in a bowl. True, it's quite a lumpy purée, but that's perfect – a few small banana lumps add texture and pockets of extra flavour.

In a separate bowl, lightly whisk the eggs with a fork. Now – and you can sense what's coming – combine the banana purée with the whisked eggs, add the salt and blend with the fork. *Voilà!* That's the pancake mixture …

Heat a splash of oil or 2 teaspoons of the butter, if using, in a large frying pan (or crêpe pan) on a medium heat. To make the first crêpe, ladle the mixture from the bowl to the hot pan and fry for 1–2 minutes on each side, reducing the heat a little, if necessary. Fold the crêpe with a spatula or palette knife and transfer it to a warm plate while you make more with the remaining mixture. Add a little more oil or butter to the pan as you go. Serve with the berries and lemon halves and, if you wish, honey or maple syrup or a light dusting of icing sugar.

Granola Bars

PREP 15 MINS / COOK 20 MINS / COOL 1 HOUR

I remember vividly making these granola bars for the first time. That was when I decided to completely reinvent breakfast at Le Manoir. Well, it took us months to accomplish the perfect organic breakfast and, by then, I'd baked so much granola that I was baking it in my dreams. At last, I was happy with this recipe. Since then we have been making and serving this granola every day, and it's much loved. I beg you to set aside about 40 minutes to make these bars just once … and then you'll be making them for years to come (and sharing the recipe). The bars will keep in an airtight container for up to 3 days (or freeze them), but they won't last that long, I promise. I like to use organic nuts, berries and oats.

MAKES 12–14 BARS (OR AT LEAST 24 BITE-SIZED PIECES)

75g pecan nuts
75g pistachio nuts
50g flaked almonds
125g jumbo oats
40g dried cranberries
40g sultanas (I like golden sultanas)
45g light brown sugar
40ml warm water
60g unsalted butter, cut into cubes
45ml honey (I like Manuka honey)

VARIATION

Many other nuts, seeds and dried fruit can be used, so please experiment with the recipe to find your favourite mix (but keep to the total weight of nuts and dried fruit, which is 280g).

Preheat the oven to 180°C/160°C fan/gas 4.

TO PREPARE Coarsely chop the pecans, pistachios and almonds.

Transfer the nuts and oats to a large, clean baking tray and spread out evenly. Bake for 8 minutes, then transfer the lightly toasted nuts and oats to a large bowl, but leave the oven on. Add the cranberries and the sultanas to the bowl, stir and put the bowl to one side.

In a medium-sized saucepan on a medium heat, bring the sugar and water to the boil and cook it to a hot, golden, bubbling caramel.

Remove the pan from the heat and immediately add the butter pieces to the hot caramel. Swirl the pan so the butter is fully incorporated. Add the honey and return the pan to a low heat. Gently warm the caramel for a minute or two until it is silky smooth. Swirl the pan and remove it from the heat. Pour this hot caramel mixture over the granola mix. Mix well, ensuring that every berry, sultana, oat and nut is caramel-coated.

Evenly spread the sticky mixture onto a small baking tray (approx. 20cm x 25cm) lined with baking parchment. With a spatula, press down quite firmly to evenly flatten the mixture.

At this stage you can either make slightly gooey granola bars, which are perfect for snacks, or you can make crunchy, brittle granola, which crumbles easily and can be added to yoghurt.

For slightly gooey granola bars, bake for 5–6 minutes. Remove the tray from the oven and leave to cool for at least 1 hour before transferring to a board. Cut it into 12 to 14 equal-sized rectangles or halve them for bite-sized squares.

For crunchy, brittle granola, simply turn off the oven after 6 minutes, but leave the tray in the oven for an hour to cool in the residual heat. This granola can be broken into clusters or mismatched bite-sized pieces.

Blueberry Buttermilk Pancakes

PREP 10 MINS / COOK 15 MINS

Whoosh! You and I are at a table in a diner, downtown in any city in the States. Waiters and waitresses whizz about with coffee jugs. There's a jukebox in the corner, and we feel like extras in a Hollywood movie … Will you join me in a plate of buttermilk pancakes? If, like me, you are in love with blueberries, then this is a must-make breakfast or brunch. You can also cook down 200g blueberries in a saucepan and serve them with these flavoursome, crispy-edged pancakes. Either way, a trickle of maple syrup seems essential.

MAKES 10 MINI PANCAKES

300ml whole milk
½ lemon
200g self-raising flour
1 teaspoon baking powder
pinch of sea salt flakes
1 heaped tablespoon
  caster sugar
1 medium egg (preferably
  organic or free-range)
25g unsalted butter
200g blueberries
sunflower oil (or use
  unsalted butter, if you
  prefer), for frying

To serve
maple syrup or crème
  fraîche or a light dusting
  of icing sugar

First, make the buttermilk. In a jug or bowl, simply combine the milk with the juice of the lemon half. Leave it for 10 minutes, and observe a small miracle – in this short time the milk will curdle, creating buttermilk that's ready to use. It will add wonderful acidity to these mini pancakes.

In a large bowl, mix together the flour, baking powder, salt and sugar. Make a well in the centre of the mixture. Lightly beat the egg and pour it into the well, followed by the buttermilk. Whisk the mixture to a smooth batter. Melt the butter and whisk it in. Finally, fold in the blueberries. That's the blueberry pancake batter (and it can be refrigerated until required).

Heat 1 tablespoon of the oil in a large non-stick frying pan on a medium heat. Let it pick up some heat – you might see a light haze above the pan – and now you can begin to cook …

Cook the mini pancakes in batches of three, using about half a ladle of batter for each pancake. Leave space between each pancake so that you can flip them. Fry on one side for 2–3 minutes and, with a spatula or palette knife, turn each pancake and fry for a further 2–3 minutes.

Transfer the cooked pancakes to a plate lined with kitchen paper. Wipe the frying pan clean with kitchen paper if necessary, and repeat with the rest of the batter until you have cooked all the pancakes (or refrigerate the remaining batter until required).

Arrange the pancakes onto plates – or stack them, diner-style. Serve with maple syrup, crème fraîche or a light dusting of icing sugar.

VARIATION

The blueberries can be substituted with many other fruits, such as raspberries, strawberries, cherries.

RB's Brown Sauce

PREP 20 MINS / COOK 1½ HOURS / COOL 1 HOUR 10 MINUTES

I never liked brown sauce. But that all changed one day when I went fishing for trout … Now, fishing is one of my great pleasures in life. Sitting by the riverbank, I truly relax and let go. I cast my line, watch the fly dancing over the ripples, and I float into an almost-meditative state. I suppose I'm not so much Fisherman's Friend, as friend of the fish. Where was I …? Oh yes. So come late morning, I left the bank, went back to my friend's house and was greeted by the sizzle and smell of bacon in the pan. 'Would you like a bacon butty?' I was asked. I nodded, but was mystified. What was this 'butty'? Well, a moment later I was devouring it – layers of crispy rashers, smothered in brown sauce and sandwiched between a couple of pieces of cheap, white processed bread. My God, it was gorgeous. I fell in love and vowed, 'Soon, I'll make my own brown sauce!' I kept the promise, and the fruity, piquant sauce has become quite famous at Brasserie Blanc. Next, the bigwigs at HP sent me a very special bottle – embossed with 'RB', and with a handsome silver lid. *Alors* – that's my brown sauce story. This recipe is a tasty way of using up the last of the season's fruit or any windfall apples that you find (first, remove any bruised parts of the apple). The Bramley, which I have vilified so often, is the best variety, bringing acidity, bulk and flavour. Brown sauce can also be used as a marinade, or as an ingredient to enrich a sauce.

MAKES 1 LITRE SAUCE

200g pitted dates
about 700g Bramley apples
1 teaspoon ground allspice
1 teaspoon ground ginger
a few gratings of nutmeg
140g dark brown sugar
200ml red wine vinegar

TO PREPARE Finely chop the dates and place them in a large ovenproof bowl. Finely dice the apples and add them to the bowl.

Add the ground allspice, ginger and nutmeg to the bowl and mix well. Reserve.

Place a saucepan over a high heat and bring the dark brown sugar and vinegar to the boil, stirring to dissolve the sugar.

Remove the pan from the heat and pour the mixture onto the chopped dates and apple in the bowl. Cover the bowl and leave to cool at room temperature for about 1 hour, until the dates have softened.

Transfer the mixture to a heavy-based saucepan and simmer over a very low heat for 1½ hours, stirring occasionally so it doesn't catch on the base. Once cooked, it will be soft and pulpy.

Leave it to cool for about 10 minutes. In a food processor or with a stick blender, blend until it's smooth. Leave it to cool completely.

Refrigerate in airtight, sterilised jars or bottles until needed, or for up to 2 months.

Aubergine and Ricotta Tartine

PREP 15 MINS / COOK 20 MINS

As a self-taught, young chef, I loved the versatility of aubergine. For one of my first dishes, I pushed a fork into an aubergine and cooked it over a high flame. Soon the heat charred the skin and penetrated the flesh. Within 10 minutes, it was blackened all over. I left it to cool a little and then sliced it open to discover the flesh – now soft and creamy-white – was wonderfully smoky and so tasty. This pride at my eureka moment vanished when I learnt this technique was almost as old as the world, originating from the Middle East. Moving on … Here is an improvement on a recipe that I wrote years ago. The aubergine pulp works so well with ricotta cheese, honey and grilled tomatoes, served on toast, tartine-style. Enjoy it as a light lunch, starter or satisfying brunch.

SERVES 4

4 large plum tomatoes
20 basil leaves
250g ricotta cheese
2 aubergines
50ml extra-virgin olive
 oil, plus extra for
 the aubergine
sea salt flakes and
 black pepper
½ lemon
1 tablespoon honey
1 tablespoon white
 wine vinegar
4 slices of rye,
 sourdough or your
 favourite good-quality
 bread

TO PREPARE Cut each tomato into six petals. Finely chop the basil leaves, reserving eight nice leaves to finish the dish. Drain the water from the ricotta, break the cheese into bite-sized pieces and reserve.

You have three options when it comes to cooking the aubergines. They can be done on a griddle pan, over a high heat. They can be cooked directly on a high gas flame, just as I did in my eureka moment. Or, more simply, place them under a grill for a total of 10 minutes, turning occasionally. Whichever way you choose, cook them until they are blackened all over. Place on kitchen paper and let them rest for at least 10 minutes.

Meanwhile, drizzle the tomatoes with extra-virgin olive oil and season with salt and a few turns of black pepper. Put them to one side. Preheat the grill to high – ready to grill the tomato petals.

Now, return to the aubergines. With the aubergines on kitchen paper, slice each one in half, butterfly-style, so that you don't entirely cut through it. With a spoon, scoop out and discard the strips of seeds. Next, scoop out the flesh. Do this carefully, so as not to remove the blackened skin in the process. Move quite quickly, to stop the flesh browning. Put this pulp in a bowl and treat it to a few strong squeezes of lemon, which will prevent it browning. Leave the pulp to cool before crushing it with a fork or blending it to a purée with a stick blender. Return it to the bowl.

Add the chopped basil, honey and white wine vinegar. Season with salt and black pepper to your taste, and add a little extra-virgin olive oil, if required. Reserve.

Place the tomatoes on a baking tray, and then grill for 4–5 minutes.

Toast the bread. Spread the aubergine mixture on each slice. Sprinkle over the ricotta, top with the separated grilled tomatoes and basil leaves, grind over some black pepper and serve.

My love for
AUBERGINES

Aubergine (or eggplant, as some know it) did not feature in the food of my childhood; what was not grown in Franche-Comté never strayed into Franche-Comté. Aubergine belongs to sunny Provence. My God, I have since made up for that aubergine absence. After I opened my first restaurant, Les Quat'Saisons in Oxford, this fruit was always on the menu when it was in season.

Today at Le Manoir we grow about a dozen varieties, trialling every year as we look for the best in taste and texture. It is this constant love, curiosity and attention that leads to the evolution of a dish. I'm embarrassed to say that, year after year, the winner is a variety called Money Maker. Whether it is young and small or older and larger, this variety is packed with flavour (when large it is firm, tight, creamy and tasty with very few seeds).

But before the cooking, there is the shopping. May I share a few tips. You see, there is the good aubergine and the not-so-good aubergine. Good is not about size, but appearance, weight and texture. I have found that often a good aubergine is not just purple, but such a dark shade of purple so as to be almost jet black. And then – crucially – it should feel heavy. That's when you know that the flesh is still filled with moisture, and it is ripe and fresh. The best way to know if you have a good aubergine is to hold it in your hand and knock it like you would knock on a door. If the aubergine is light and the sound is hollow, then it is overripe with lots of seeds and pockets of air. If the sound is a flat thud and the aubergine is heavy, you know you are heading towards aubergine heaven.

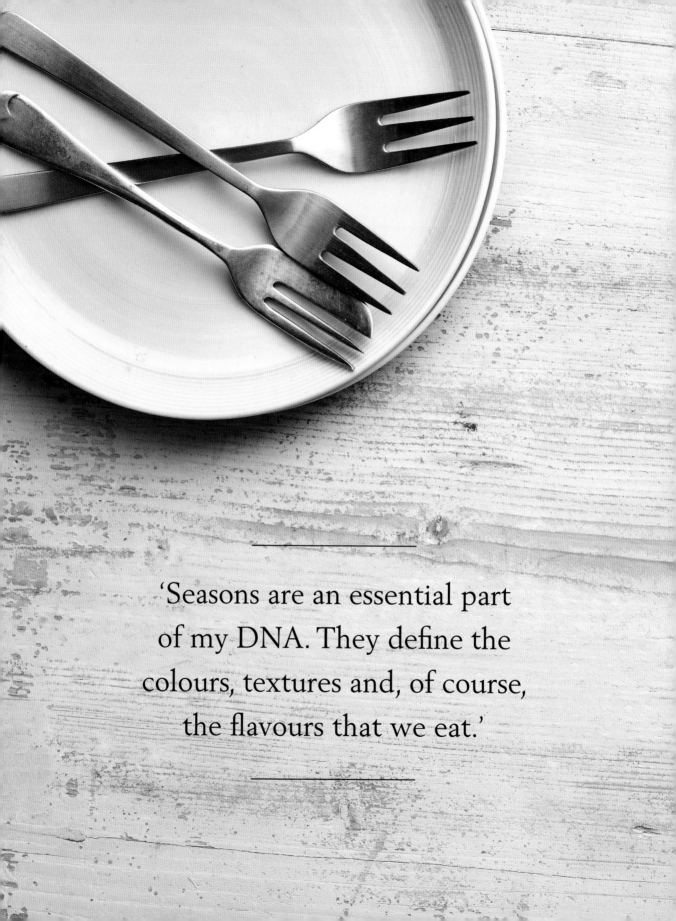

'Seasons are an essential part
of my DNA. They define the
colours, textures and, of course,
the flavours that we eat.'

LES PETITS PLATS

Fast Flatbreads
52

Vegetable Samosas
55

Polenta Cake
56

Assiette de Crudités,
Maman Blanc
59

My Love for Beetroot
60

Falafel with Chickpea
Mayonnaise
62

Cornbread Loaf
64

Rosemary and Parmesan Popcorn

PREP 3 MINS / COOK 5 MINS

I love the mystique of popcorn. I have created some crazy dishes in my time, but had never made it, so it remained a mystery to me. At Le Manoir I had grown half a dozen rows of maize, and was looking forward to popping the corn. Alas, it was the wrong variety and could not pop. I was disappointed, but delighted with the Cornbread (see page 64). Undeterred, I found the right variety in a supermarket and then finally got to make popcorn. So why does it pop? There's a minute droplet of water in the corn's kernels that heat transforms into steam. Each kernel is like a tiny pressure cooker. Suddenly, the vapour bursts through the skin and the kernel acts like an echo chamber … pop, pop, pop! How fantastic that simply through the application of heat these corns explode into a miraculous, mini snack of snowy-white beauties, perfect with drinks before a meal. And all in less than 10 minutes. For me, it's been a huge discovery, and now will be served in every one of my Brasserie Blanc restaurants.

MAKES ENOUGH FOR 4–6

100g Parmigiano-
 Reggiano cheese
4 small rosemary sprigs
2 tablespoons
 sunflower oil
250g popping corn
2 pinches of sea salt
 flakes
30g unsalted butter,
 melted
pinch of cayenne pepper

TO PREPARE Finely grate the cheese and put it to one side. Chop the rosemary into smaller sprigs (or break each sprig in half).

Heat the oil in a large heavy-based saucepan on a medium–high heat, add the popping corn, salt and rosemary and immediately cover the pan with a lid. Wait, wait, wait and let the popping commence … Cook for 3–5 minutes, shaking the pan every 20 seconds to assist the popping and stop the corn burning.

Remove the pan from the heat. Transfer the popcorn to a large serving bowl using a spider or slotted spoon and shake the pan, leaving the un-popped kernels to fall to the bottom. While the popcorn is still hot, cover it with the melted butter, cheese and cayenne pepper. Serve immediately, while it is warm, herby, salty, buttery and crunchy.

VARIATIONS

• Replace the rosemary with other fresh herbs or lemon zest.

• Try smoked paprika instead of cayenne pepper.

Flash-fried Padrón Peppers

PREP 5 MINS / COOK 5 MINS

These dinky green peppers come from Padrón in Galicia, in the northwestern corner of Spain. The only issue with these little peppers is that their DNA means one out of twenty or so will give a serious burst of spice. You can add any spices to this dish, such as your favourite curry powder. Flash-fried to a lovely crunch in just a few minutes, they are an easy tapas or canapé and superb with a glass of chilled rosé, white wine, sparkling wine or a cold beer.

SERVES 4

24 Padrón peppers
3 tablespoons olive oil
4 generous pinches
   of ground cumin
pinch of sea salt flakes
2 turns of ground
   black pepper

In a large bowl, mix the peppers with the oil so that they are well coated. Heat a large frying pan or wok on a high heat. When the pan is very hot, add the peppers and flash-fry them for 2–3 minutes, tossing once or twice.

Remove the pan from the heat, sprinkle with the cumin, salt and pepper and toss the ingredients. That's all that is needed!

Transfer the flash-fried peppers to a large bowl and serve them while hot to your family and friends.

VARIATIONS

• Add a handful of mangetout or sugar snap peas with the peppers.

• Add 6 okra with the peppers. Remove and discard the hard tips and cut each okra into pieces about ½cm thick.

• Alternatively, add a dozen red and yellow cherry tomatoes or 1 courgette, sliced lengthways and diced, with the peppers.

• Add a few celery leaves with the cumin.

My love for
PEPPERS

I adore the sweet pepper, or bell pepper as the Americans know it. It is indeed bell-shaped (so perfect for stuffing) and it is sweet (so great for salads), as well as being crunchy and tasty. It is no relation to pepper the spice, but instead a member of the capsicum Solanaceae genus. Which means it's related to the potato and tomato and originates from the Americas. Red is stunning, and the green pepper is usually – but not always – an unripe red pepper, though with its own distinctive taste. Red, green, yellow or golden, this type of pepper is a beautiful work of art.

At Le Manoir, Anne-Marie and her team of gardeners tend to a dozen varieties of peppers, giving us a wonderful range of pepper taste, texture and colour. For bell peppers, I like a golden variety called Californian Golden, which may come from America's sunshine state but seems to have adapted to the weather of Oxfordshire. So you may wish to grow them at home. To do so, on a day in February take the seeds from a pepper and plant them in a pot. Keep the pot indoors, snug and warm. A plant will grow. I hope. Come May, transfer the plant to your garden and watch as it flourishes.

If you do end up with a glut of homegrown peppers, or with too many in your fridge, dice them or slice them and store them in the freezer. That way you can use them, straight from the freezer and still frozen, in stir-fries and curries. To add a more authentic smoky flavour to your casserole, chilli or curry, first sear the prepared peppers in a hot, dry frying pan, charring the skin of the peppers. This will impart more flavour to your dishes.

Consider, too, the health benefits of the pepper. It is crammed with nutrients, such as vitamins C, A and B6. And it is rich in carotenoids, the antioxidants that help protect cells from oxidative damage.

Smoked Haddock Beignets

PREP 10 MINS / COOK 25 MINS

These small pieces of battered fish are extremely popular, and a pleasure to make. They are both flaky and meaty. I like them as a starter, but if you are serving them as a main course for four, increase the amount of fish to 600g. The beignets can be cooked in hot oil in a deep fryer or shallow-fried in a deep-sided sauté pan. Meanwhile, the haddock pieces can be marinated and refrigerated up to 4 hours before cooking. Serve with lemon wedges and the chive mayonnaise below or your choice of Tartare Sauce or Sauce Gribiche (see page 293). A little bit of indulgence has never harmed anyone.

MAKES 32 BEIGNETS

500g smoked haddock
   fillets, skin removed
2 sprigs of dill
juice of ½ lemon
1 tablespoon Dijon
   mustard
2 turns of ground
   black pepper
vegetable oil, for frying
sea salt flakes

For the beignet batter
1 medium egg yolk
   (preferably organic
   or free-range)
35g unsalted butter,
   melted
180g plain flour
225ml beer (or lager
   or sparkling water)
2 medium egg whites
   (preferably organic
   or free-range)

For the chive mayonnaise
6 tablespoons
   mayonnaise (shop-
   bought or see my
   recipe on page 111)
1 tablespoon finely
   chopped chives

TO PREPARE Cut each haddock fillet into chunky bite-sized pieces and transfer them to a bowl (or tray). Finely chop the dill.

Marinate the fish with the lemon juice, mustard, dill and pepper. Toss the fish pieces to incorporate the flavours. Put the fish to one side while you make the batter or, if you want to cook this later, cover the bowl with non-pvc clingfilm and refrigerate until ready (for up to 4 hours).

Combine the egg yolk and melted butter in a large bowl and whisk in the flour, little by little. Now add the beer to thin it. Separately whisk the egg whites to a light, foamy stage and fold them into the batter to lighten it.

Heat the oil in a large deep-sided sauté pan (or if using a deep fryer, please be cautious and heat it to 170°C/340°F). Check the oil is hot enough by spooning a drop of batter into the oil – if it sizzles, *c'est bon* and it's time to fry.

Cook the smoked haddock pieces in batches of four to six, depending on the size of the pan. Dip the pieces into the batter to coat them and transfer them with a slotted spoon to the hot oil. Fry the pieces, turning once, for 3–4 minutes, or until the batter is perfectly crisp and they are golden.

Drain the beignets on kitchen paper and lightly season them with salt. Mix the mayonnaise and chives together and serve with the beignets.

VARIATIONS

• Why not add your favourite spices, seeds or herbs to the batter?

• The smoked haddock can be substituted with other white flaky-fleshed fish, such as cod, pollock or halibut.

• If you fancy a bit more fun, dip sprigs of parsley or coriander in the batter and deep-fry them before the fish.

Mini Potato Pancakes

PREP 10 MINS / COOK 10 MINS (OR 30 MINS IF COOKING POTATOES)

Mashing is a personal thing, isn't it? We all have our own techniques and gadgets for the job, some good, others bad. There are those who swear by the 'ricer', though most British cooks favour the masher. As a Frenchman, I use my moulin-légumes (the holes are ideally sized for mashing and don't make the potato glutenous). Whatever the tool, the aim is the same: mashed potato must always be fluffy and light, never overworked and gloopy. Mashing is a gentle process, requiring only a little milk, white pepper and butter, but no, not too much. Regardless of the tool, it is the potato that matters the most. Of the easily available varieties, I like Maris Piper and King Edward. I also recommend Bintje. These little golden pancakes are a bit like blinis: warm, soft and more-ish. They can be a snack or served as canapés, topped with grated cheese, smoked salmon or crème fraîche and chives. Or enjoy them for brunch, served with poached eggs and wilted spinach.

SERVES AT LEAST 4

350g Maris Piper
    potatoes (or cooked
    leftover mashed
    potatoes)
100g good-quality slices
    of ham (optional)
3 medium eggs
    (preferably organic
    or free-range)
40g plain flour
70ml whole milk
70ml double cream
2 generous pinches of
    sea salt flakes
2 turns of ground white
    pepper
pinch of freshly grated
    nutmeg (optional)
a handful of finely
    chopped chives
    (optional)
25g unsalted butter

TO PREPARE Well done if you are making these pancakes with leftover mash. You've saved some time, but do warm it before mixing to make the pancakes. If you need to make the mash, peel, quarter and rinse the potatoes. If using ham, roll each ham slice and chop it into julienne strips.

Place the potatoes in a large saucepan of boiling, salted water. After about 20 minutes on a fast simmer, test them with the tip of a knife. Drain, mash and allow them to cool a little.

In a large bowl and using a spatula, combine the mashed potatoes with the eggs, flour, milk and cream. Season with the sea salt, white pepper and, if using, a little grated nutmeg. (At this stage the batter can be covered with non-pvc clingfilm and refrigerated for up to 1 day.) If using, stir the chives and ham into the mixture before cooking.

In a large – and preferably non-stick – sauté pan or frying pan, melt 1–2 teaspoons of the butter on a medium heat. Use a pastry brush to coat the pan with the hot butter. When the butter begins to foam, start to make the pancakes in batches of six to seven, using a dessertspoon as a mini ladle to transfer the batter to the hot pan. Fry the pancakes for about 1 minute on each side, or until golden, turning with a spatula or palette knife. Remove the pancakes from the pan onto a plate and keep somewhere warm until you have cooked all the mix. Repeat the process, adding more butter to the pan, as required.

VARIATION

Steam finely sliced leek or cabbage in a pan with a little water and a knob of butter. Mix the cooked vegetables into the pancake mixture – mini French bubble and squeak!

Tuna Ceviche, Japanese-style

PREP 10 MINS / MARINATE 5 MINS

Ceviche is the Peruvian way of preparing raw fish in citrus juice, often lime. So it sounds odd to place ceviche close to Japan. But while this dish is heavily inspired by Peru and South America, I have incorporated distinctly Asian flavours, such as soy, mirin and mooli (also known as daikon radish). And actually, every country has its own take on ceviche; an illustration of how, over the years, culinary ideas and dishes travel across the world. This little summer starter is refreshing, delicious and fun to make. The freshness of the ingredients is crucial, and while this dish has a little bit of refinement, sometimes it's important to show off a bit.

SERVES 4

2 tuna steaks (each
　approx. 150g)
100g mooli (daikon)
　radish
4–6 coriander sprigs
　(optional)
1 spring onion
1 lime
1 tablespoon dark soy
　sauce
3 teaspoons mirin
20g dulse seaweed
　(optional)
a handful of celery
　leaves, to garnish

TO PREPARE Using a sharp knife, dice the tuna steaks into cubes of about 1–1½cm and place in a medium-sized mixing bowl. Peel and halve the mooli lengthways and finely slice it. Pick the coriander leaves from their stalks, if using, and chop the leaves and stalks into about 1cm pieces. Finely chop the spring onion.

Squeeze the juice of the lime over the tuna and toss, then leave for 5 minutes. Next, add the soy and mirin (the mirin sweetens and tempers the acidity of the lime juice). Toss once more.

Add the mooli to the tuna mix with the coriander, spring onion and seaweed, if using. Toss all the ingredients.

Divide the marinated tuna into four shallow bowls. Scatter each bowl with a few leaves of celery and serve.

VARIATIONS

• To this summer treat you could add so many other flavours and textures. Before serving, add 100ml cold dashi stock or miso soup to each bowl.

• The tuna can be substituted with many other fish and shellfish, including mackerel, salmon, lobster, scallops and prawns (or a mixture).

• Add mint or chives, mustard leaves or garlic. For heat, add a grating of ginger or wasabi.

• Instead of mooli, try bamboo shoots or palm hearts.

Broad Beans with Parmesan, and a Joke

PREP 1 MIN / COOK 5 MINS, IF YOU TAKE YOUR TIME

With my amazing team at Le Manoir, our aim is to give the best, the sublime. Le Manoir touches all the notes of excellence, often with complex, refined dishes. It's a gastronomic opera, but when I head home, usually I fancy wholesome, rustic food. For some chefs, that late-night snack is a bacon sandwich or baked beans on toast. I crave simplicity and Natalia, my partner, takes care of that. Besides her endless patience, she is kind enough to insist on cooking this late-night dish, which never fails to delight. It's a wonderful ritual. Of course, I am able to cook my own broad beans, but she does this dish the best, and out of season uses beans straight from the freezer. It is light, simple, and Natalia serves it with a great joke to lighten a tough day. I am a very lucky man and her food is always appreciated. I'd never dare complain, and anyway there's no reason to. Afterwards, the ritual continues. I move on to a little slice of rye or sourdough bread and a tiny bit of goat's cheese, as well as one glass – or maybe two – of Guillaume Pinot Noir. These beans can also accompany Natalia's Pan-fried Slip Sole (see page 149).

SERVES 2

1 garlic clove
about 300g broad beans, frozen (or fresh)
a large handful of spinach (optional)
3 tablespoons extra-virgin olive oil, plus extra to finish
sea salt flakes and black pepper
100ml water
a strong squeeze of lemon juice
a few generous gratings of Parmigiano-Reggiano cheese (or Cheddar or Comté)

To serve
1 joke, to your taste

TO PREPARE First, finely slice the peeled garlic. Please leave the skins on the beans for extra flavour, texture and fibre. Wash and dry the spinach, if using. Your preparation is done. Exhausting, *non?*

Put the beans, sliced garlic and extra-virgin olive oil into a medium-sized saucepan. Season to your taste with the salt and pepper and add the water. Over a high heat, bring to a full boil and let the water evaporate as the beans warm through.

Stir in the spinach and add a strong squeeze of lemon.

If the beans are frozen, it will take 4–5 minutes of your time. If the beans are fresh, only 2–3 minutes to cook.

Add generous gratings of cheese, transfer to a bowl and pour over a dash of extra-virgin oil. Serve with a joke, and enjoy. Thank you, Natalia.

Fast Flatbreads

PREP 5 MINS / COOK 15 MINS

This is bread-making in its simplest and most ancient form. Just three ingredients: yoghurt, flour and salt. And with equal quantities of the yoghurt and flour – weigh both ingredients in the same bowl, and the next time you make the dough you can use the bowl rather than the scales. The flatbreads can be thin, like wraps. Or make them thick, like pizza bases, to be smothered while hot with crushed avocado, houmous, olive tapenade, tomato passata, crushed garlic or olive oil and balsamic … they are blank canvases upon which you, the artist, can create culinary masterpieces with your favourite vegetables, herbs, seeds or cheese. You could try a topping of rocket and feta or houmous, cucumber, courgette and garlic. Or serve them with A Quick Ratatouille on page 195. Make these flatbreads just once, and you'll make them many more times …

MAKES 4 THIN FLATBREADS OR 2 THICKER ONES

120g self-raising flour, plus extra for dusting
120g natural yoghurt (or skyr, the Icelandic-style yoghurt)
a generous pinch of sea salt flakes

In a large bowl, mix together the flour, yoghurt and salt to form a smooth ball of dough. You can certainly do this with your hands, which is a little messy but highly rewarding. Otherwise, a spatula will do very well.

Lightly flour a large board or work surface. Divide the dough into four pieces – each about the same size. (For thicker, pizza-style flatbreads, divide the dough in half.)

Put one piece of dough on the floured surface. Use a rolling pin to roll the dough to the thickness of a thin pancake or simply flatten out the dough by patting it with the palm of your hand. Try to form a round flatbread that won't be too large for your pan. But if the flatbread dough is too thick, or not round, please don't worry.

Put a large frying or crêpe pan on a medium–high heat and give it a moment or two to pick up some heat. Place one piece of flattened dough into the hot pan. (Note: it's a dry pan, there's no hissing oil or sizzling butter, and when you've finished, it only needs a wipe with a cloth.)

VARIATIONS

So many other flavours can be added to the dough, such as coriander, chopped chilli, black onion seeds and smoked paprika.

Cook for 1–2 minutes until it's browned, and then use a spatula or palette knife to turn and cook it for a further 1–2 minutes. Both sides should be browned, a bit bumpy and mottled. Turn one final time, and the flatbread will have a pleasing rise in the middle – it won't be so flat, after all.

Remove the flatbread from the pan and keep it to one side while you make more flatbreads with the remaining dough. After a couple, you'll be making your flatbreads exactly the way you like them – thick or thin, soft and ideal for a wrap, or with slightly charred and crunchy edges … Serve the flatbreads hot or warm, but they are also delicious at room temperature.

Vegetable Samosas

PREP 25 MINS / COOK 40 MINS / CHILL 1 HOUR

I met samosas on my travels, fell in love with them, and then Clive and I put them on the menu at Brasserie Blanc. Crispy, spicy, crunchy, flaky, they can be served as canapés, snacks, a starter or main course. Or simply make the filling as an accompaniment to Cauliflower and Red Lentil Dhal (see page 192). Here the parcels are baked in the final stage, but you can deep-fry or shallow-fry them.

MAKES AT LEAST 12 SAMOSAS

150g potatoes
1 small onion
½ red chilli
2 garlic cloves
1cm piece of fresh
   root ginger
2 tablespoons sunflower
   oil, plus extra for
   bonding the pastry
½ teaspoon fennel seeds
1 teaspoon ground cumin
1 teaspoon curry powder
2 pinches of sea salt flakes
150g peas
½ lemon, for squeezing
1 packet (about 250g)
   filo pastry

To serve
mango chutney
natural yoghurt
a sprinkling of sliced
   chives
a sprinkling of
   pomegranate seeds
   (optional)

TO PREPARE Peel and quarter the potatoes. Finely dice the onion and finely chop the red chilli. Crush the peeled garlic cloves with the back of a knife to make a paste. Grate the peeled ginger. That's the preparation, now for the cooking …

Cook the potatoes in gently boiling, salted water for 15–20 minutes or until just tender. Mash and put to one side to cool.

Heat a large sauté pan or frying pan with the oil on a medium heat, add the fennel seeds and lightly fry them for about 30 seconds. Add the onion, stir, and continue to fry for 3–4 minutes, until softened. Add the chilli, garlic, ginger, cumin, curry powder and salt. Cover the pan with a lid and cook for 4 minutes, stirring a few times to prevent the ingredients sticking to the pan or burning. Add the peas and cook for 1 more minute.

Remove the pan from the heat, add the mashed potato and stir well. Taste and adjust the seasoning with a little lemon juice and add more salt, if required. Allow the mixture to cool slightly.

Next, the parcels. Start by cutting a sheet of filo pastry in half lengthways. Put one of the halves aside. With the half that's on the board, place about a dessertspoonful of the samosa mix close to the top left-hand corner of the pastry sheet. Next, lift the top left corner of the sheet and fold it over the mixture, creating a triangle shape. Repeat this process, folding the parcel as you move from left to right. Continue to fold until the sheet is no more. Once you've made the parcel, use only a brush of oil to bond the pastry. Place the parcel on a tray.

Repeat the process, to make at least eleven more samosas with the remaining filling and pastry. Put them on the tray as you go. Place the tray of samosas in the fridge for an hour so that they firm up before cooking.

When it's time to cook, preheat the oven to 180°C/160°C fan/gas 4.

Brush each samosa with a little oil and bake for about 7–8 minutes, then turn them over and bake for a further 6–7 minutes or until golden. Leave them to cool for a few minutes before serving. Serve with mango chutney, some yoghurt sprinkled with chives and pomegranate seeds.

Polenta Cake

PREP 10 MINS / COOK 10 MINS / COOL 15 MINS / CHILL 2 HOURS

Polenta is ground from corn and has long been a staple of Italy and Latin America, and is often an ingredient in pasta. It can be made into a vegan cake, too, which is freezeable. Like bread, toast or pizza, these polenta cake slices can be a base for toppings. Try with A Quick Ratatouille (see page 195) or enjoy the cake topped with a poached egg and wilted spinach or layered with olive tapenade, finely chopped tomatoes and herbs. In this recipe, the sun-dried tomatoes can be substituted for more olives and vice versa. Or use Oven-dried Tomatoes and Olives (see page 291).

SERVES AT LEAST 4 (MAKES 6–10 SLICES)

3 tablespoons dried black olives

a handful of sun-dried tomatoes

2 garlic cloves

a small handful of flat-leaf parsley

600ml water

40ml olive oil, plus a little extra for greasing the tin and frying

200g polenta

4 pinches of sea salt flakes

2 turns of ground black pepper

TO PREPARE Lightly brush oil over a medium-sized, straight-sided baking tray (or another shallow dish). Line the tray with non-pvc clingfilm and put it to one side. Coarsely chop the olives and tomatoes. Use the back of a knife or a fine grater to crush the peeled garlic to a paste. Finely chop the parsley. Put all of these to one side.

Pour the water and olive oil into a large saucepan and, on a high heat, bring to the boil and then add the polenta, salt and pepper. Bring the water back up to the boil and stir continuously with a whisk for 2–3 minutes. Notice how the polenta quickly thickens as it absorbs the water and oil. If the polenta bubbles and spits, just reduce the heat a little.

Remove the pan from the heat and – while the polenta is still piping hot – add the olives, sun-dried tomatoes, garlic and parsley. Stir well.

Spoon the mixture into the lined tray and flatten it evenly with a spatula. The polenta doesn't need to fill the whole surface of the tin but it should be as deep as a very thick slice of bread (about 2½cm).

Lightly cover the polenta with clingfilm and leave it to cool for 15 minutes before transferring it to the fridge for at least 2 hours. When it's time to serve, turn out the chilled polenta cake onto a board and slice the cake into portions. You can cut small or big squares, or use a pastry cutter or upturned cup to create polenta cake circles.

In a frying pan, on a medium heat, fry the polenta slices in olive oil for 2–3 minutes. Turn and fry for a further 2 minutes, or until golden all over.

AVOCADO DIP

Spoon out the flesh of 2 medium-sized ripe (they must be ripe) avocados. Crush the flesh with the back of a fork and add a few squeezes of lemon juice. Combine with extra-virgin olive oil until shiny and smooth. Add a pinch of cayenne pepper, stir, taste and check the seasoning. Gently warm the avocado mixture in a saucepan, and serve it as a dip with the polenta cake.

Assiette de Crudités, Maman Blanc

PREP 1 HOUR / COOK 10 MINS, PLUS 1½ HOURS FOR THE BEETROOT

While the mighty roast beef is being relished by my British friends, crudités are served in lots of homes in France every Sunday. Maman Blanc would make it as the prelude to a big lunch with extended family. A colourful, delicious celebration of the garden, it can be as simple as you want, such as grated carrot or celeriac with hard-boiled eggs and a mustard dressing.

SERVES 4–6

4 beetroot
4 medium eggs
  (preferably organic
  or free-range)
150g French beans
400g celeriac
3 tablespoons lemon juice
1 large cucumber
4 big, fat ripe tomatoes
2 large carrots
1 large lettuce (I like
  Reine des Glaces –
  Queen of the Ices)

For the dressing
4 banana shallots
40g Dijon mustard
25ml white wine vinegar
40ml warm water
150ml groundnut oil
  (or vegetable or
  sunflower oil)
sea salt flakes and
  black pepper

TO PREPARE Begin by washing and trimming the beetroot. Place them in a large saucepan and cover with water. Over a high heat, bring to the boil and then reduce to a simmer and cook like this for 1½ hours (if you prefer, the beetroot can be steamed). Allow the beetroot to cool slightly before peeling them and slicing.

While the beetroot are cooking, you can prepare the other components:

Eggs: boil for 10 minutes. Cool in cold water for 1 minute, then peel while the eggs are still warm. Leave in a bowl of cold water and halve just before serving.
French beans: top and tail them. Blanch for 2 minutes in a saucepan of boiling, salted water. Drain and refresh the beans in a bowl of iced water. Drain and put them to one side.
Celeriac: peel and finely slice or coarsely grate into long strips, using a mandolin or spiralizer if you have either, and mix with 2 tablespoons of lemon juice (to stop it turning brown).
Cucumber: peel and finely slice.
Tomatoes: chop into chunky pieces (about 3cm).
Carrots: peel, grate and mix with 1 tablespoon of lemon juice to stop the carrot turning brown.
Lettuce: pick and wash.
Shallots: finely chop, wash them in a sieve under cold running water and place them on kitchen paper to dry.

To make the dressing, using a whisk combine all the dressing ingredients. Taste, and correct the seasoning if necessary.

Divide the vegetables into separate bowls and I recommend you mix them with the dressing like this:
2 tablespoons dressing with the beetroot, cucumber, tomatoes and carrots
1 tablespoon dressing with the beans
4 tablespoons dressing with the celeriac

To serve, toss the salad leaves with about 3 tablespoons of the dressing and place them on a large serving plate. Next, arrange the dressed vegetables on top of the lettuce and around the plate. Garnish with the boiled egg halves. Add a little extra dressing if necessary.

My love for
BEETROOT

When I came to Britain in the 1970s, I would talk with my new friends about the food in their lives. I discovered that they had only ever eaten beetroot when it was red, seriously overcooked and then pickled in malt vinegar. Often, I was told, 'I had it that way at school … and have avoided beetroot ever since.'

The beautiful, earthy, sweet beetroot has made much progress. It is flavoursome, does not have to be pickled and, if so, only lightly. It can be eaten hot too, and comes in colours other than ruby red. Today Britain has rediscovered the many heritage varieties, and golden beetroot, which is delicately flavoured.

It is also versatile – grated in salads, delicious in soups, roasted and served with the Sunday roast and even an ingredient in a rich chocolate cake. Beetroot also goes very well with blue cheese and nuts. In the potager at Le Manoir, they are seeded in May and take three months to reach the right size. At that point, they can remain in the ground for the whole of winter because they are frost proof and, in fact, their sweetness intensifies with the frost. Usually, I find the larger the beetroot, the tastier it is.

Do not peel or cut the beetroot when preparing, as it will lose its nutrients and colour during cooking. If cooking from raw, beetroot can take a while to cook – up to an hour of simmering in a pan of water. Using a pressure cooker will reduce the cooking time by half. Test the beetroot by inserting a small knife: it should meet with no resistance. Once the beetroot is cool enough to handle, rub off the skin. It can be marinated while still warm with chopped shallots in red or white wine vinegar, olive oil, salt and pepper. As it is warm, it will absorb lots of flavour. You may want to wear surgical gloves when preparing ruby beetroot, unless you'd like red fingers.

As for green fingers … If you are considering growing beetroot, may I recommend a few varieties: Chioggia, which has stunning rings of ruby, white and pink; Rouge Crapaudine (my favourite) and Bull's Blood.

Falafel with Chickpea Mayonnaise

This Middle Eastern savoury delight – and a popular street food in Britain – is fun to make at home. Falafel is little more than a blend of chickpeas, chickpea flour, lots of herbs and some spice, hand-rolled to make balls (or patties). You can replace the chickpeas with other beans, or use a variety. These are then deep-fried, and served with salad in Fast Flatbreads (see page 52). Sometimes the 'ball' is flattened or squashed a little before eating. The contrast of crunchy exterior and soft inside is deeply appealing. Falafel is delicious with Chickpea Mayonnaise (see recipe opposite), made with the water from the tin of chickpeas, which contains a protein that binds the sauce in place of an egg yolk. It's good to know there are alternatives to the classic sauces and our vegan friends will love this version of the traditional egg-based mayonnaise.

Falafel

PREP 15 MINS / COOK 20 MINS

MAKES ABOUT 20 FALAFEL

1 tin (400g) chickpeas
1 onion
1 garlic clove
30g curly or flat-leaf parsley
a handful of coriander (optional)
pinch of ground coriander
pinch of ground cumin
zest and juice of 1 lemon
1 teaspoon sea salt flakes
2 tablespoons extra-virgin olive oil
280g chickpea (gram) flour
sunflower oil, for frying

TO PREPARE Drain the chickpeas, keeping the water from the tin as it is an ingredient for the chickpea mayonnaise. Rinse the chickpeas. Coarsely chop the onion and peeled garlic.

In a food processor or using a stick blender, blend the chickpeas and onion with the garlic, parsley and coriander, if using, ground coriander, ground cumin, the zest and half the juice of the lemon, sea salt and oil. It shouldn't be fully blended – some lumps are ideal. Stir well and taste – add a little more salt or lemon juice, accordingly.

Transfer the mixture to a large bowl, add the chickpea flour and mix well. Hand roll equal-sized balls or patties of falafel – golf-ball sized is about right, but it's up to you, of course. Store in the fridge or freezer until required.

The falafel can be cooked in one of three ways:

1. Deep-fry: in sunflower oil (at 180°C/360°F) for 2 minutes. This is traditional and from my taste tests, it's the best method of cooking falafel. The balls cook quickly and are perfectly crunchy.

2. Shallow-fry: in sunflower oil in a frying pan for 3–4 minutes.

3. Bake in the oven: brush the falafel with a little oil and bake at 180°C/160°C fan/gas 4 until browned and crispy on the outside.

Serve the falafel with a bowl of the chickpea mayonnaise.

Chickpea Mayonnaise

PREP 10 MINS

**MAKES ENOUGH
MAYONNAISE FOR 4**

30–50ml chickpea water
   (the water from a
   tin of chickpeas)
1½ teaspoons Dijon
   mustard
150ml vegetable oil
juice of ½ lemon
pinch of sea salt flakes
small pinch of cayenne
   pepper, plus extra to
   garnish (optional)

In a medium-sized bowl, whisk the chickpea water and mustard to form a smooth emulsion. Now, whisk continuously and add the oil in a steady trickle. Let the mixture thicken to your liking (you might require a little less oil than I suggest).

Add half the lemon juice, the salt and cayenne pepper, if using. Whisk for a few seconds and taste. Add more lemon juice, to your taste, and adjust the seasoning to your liking.

If the mayonnaise seems too thick, thin it with a tablespoon or two of warm water, and then whisk once more. Cover with non-pvc clingfilm and refrigerate until needed, for up to 4 days. Serve with a sprinkling of cayenne pepper, if using.

Cornbread Loaf

PREP 10 MINS / COOK 40 MINS

We have been making this gluten-free cornbread at Le Manoir since the turn of the century. Actually, it seems like we were making it before there were any gluten-intolerant guests. Maize is a staple food of South America, and grows very well in Europe. In 2020 I had the first trial of maize at Le Manoir and … success! (Even if I couldn't make popcorn with the harvest.) The cornmeal, or polenta, became an ingredient in many recipes, including this bread. Gluten allergies often stem from modern-day wheat, which has a greater gluten content than ever before. The body has trouble breaking down these high levels of gluten. So this bread is a good offering for anyone who has a gluten intolerance. The recipe requires a tin for a 900g loaf, but is easily adapted, or make two small loaves in a couple of tins. The loaf can be made, kept in the freezer, and then defrosted as required.

SERVES 6–8

juice of ½ lemon
350ml whole milk
120g gluten-free
   bread flour
25g gluten-free
   baking powder
120g fine cornmeal
   (polenta)
2 pinches of fine salt
20g caster sugar
2 medium eggs
   (preferably organic
   or free-range)
50g unsalted butter,
   plus extra for
   greasing the tin

Preheat the oven to 175°C/155°C fan/gas 3½.

Buttermilk can be bought, but is easy to make at home. Simply squeeze the juice of the lemon half into 250ml of the milk, stir and leave for 10 minutes. The milk will curdle and is then ready to use.

Grease a 900g loaf tin, line it with a strip of greaseproof paper that will cover the bottom of the tin, the two ends of the tin and sides and grease. You will thank me for this later as this will help you to pull out the loaf when it's cooked.

Sift the flour and baking powder into a large bowl. Add the cornmeal, salt and sugar. Set aside.

In a separate bowl, whisk the buttermilk and eggs until smooth.

Next, melt the butter in a small pan over a medium heat. Make a small well in the centre of the flour-cornmeal mix. Pour in the rest of the milk, as well as the egg-buttermilk and the melted butter. Mix and then whisk (it will be a loose mixture as it is only bound by eggs).

Transfer the mixture to the lined loaf tin and bake for 40 minutes. When cooked, the loaf will be golden all over. To check, insert a skewer into the middle of the loaf – it should come out clean.

Remove the loaf from the tin and resist nibbling, which is difficult as, by now, the fantastic baking smells will have filled your home. Leave it to cool before succumbing to temptation and cutting a slice …

'Too many cooks
never make broth.
But homemade soup
is so tasty and healthy
and you can cook
it in minutes.'

SOUPS

'Maman Blanc never used stocks.
She had the deepest understanding
of food, and with water she could
transform an ingredient into the
most wholesome experience.'

Chilled Avocado Soup

PREP 10 MINS / CHILL 2 HOURS

Think of a chilled soup and gazpacho comes to mind. While we know gazpacho as a tomato soup, it was being made with other ingredients long before the first tomatoes arrived in Spain. This chilled soup is not gazpacho, but it retains a few of gazpacho's original Moorish ingredients: salt, water, garlic and vinegar (which was an essential soup ingredient for the Ancient Romans). For this soup you can do as they did, and pound the ingredients with a pestle and mortar. Or do as I do, and use a food processor. Today, we also have the freezer: this soup can be frozen in batches and defrosted fully before serving. Try it with a tiny dash of Worcestershire sauce …

SERVES 4

1 large cucumber
½ stick of celery
½ banana shallot
1 avocado
1 garlic clove
50g baby-leaf spinach
  (or sea kale)
6 coriander sprigs
2 tablespoons extra-
  virgin olive oil
100ml water
2 tablespoons white
  wine vinegar
15g caster sugar
1 teaspoon sea salt
  flakes
pinch of cayenne pepper

To finish
1 avocado
pinch of smoked paprika
  or cayenne pepper
extra-virgin olive oil

TO PREPARE Peel and coarsely chop the cucumber. Coarsely chop the celery, shallot and one of the avocados and peel the garlic. Place them all in a food processor, so that they are ready to be blended.

Add the remaining ingredients to the food processor and blend to a smooth purée. Taste and, if necessary, add a little more water, sugar or spice.

Just like revenge, this is a dish best served cold – refrigerate the soup until required, and for at least 2 hours.

Before serving, dice the remaining avocado. Divide the chilled soup into four bowls and garnish each with a soup spoon of diced avocado, a sprinkling of smoked paprika and a drizzle of your finest extra-virgin olive oil.

White Onion Soup

PREP 5 MINS / COOK 20 MINS

Hearty and heartwarming, onion soup was a staple in the chilly winter months of my childhood in Franche-Comté. Wives made it to keep their husbands going during the men-only, all-night card games of tarot. The soup pot sat there on the hob, saying to all who passed, 'Help yourself to a bowl.' And as a teenager, I'd cook onion soup for my friends, usually at around dawn – it was the nourishing pick-us-up after a night of partying. Tipsily, we'd mop our bowls with hunks of bread ripped from a crusty baguette, crumbs flying everywhere. The white onion is best for this soup. Sweeter, softer and milder than other varieties, it is also less fibrous and therefore cooks quickly. And it is not as sulphurous as its cousins, so you should not cry too much when slicing. This is a quick, easy, yummy, rustic soup, which will really put a smile on your face.

SERVES 2

4 white onions
2 garlic cloves
80g Comté cheese
  (or any hard cheese
  of your choice)
2 tablespoons unsalted
  butter
2 bay leaves
3 thyme sprigs
6 pinches of sea salt flakes
5 turns of ground black
  pepper
600ml recently boiled
  water
croutons (optional)
a handful of finely sliced
  chives (optional)

TO PREPARE First, the slicing of the onions. Chop each onion in half crossways, and then finely slice each half – not too thick, not too thin. Slice the peeled garlic and grate the Comté, then put them to one side.

Place a large heavy-based saucepan on a medium–high heat. Give it a moment to pick up some heat. Add the butter, let it foam and, before it browns, add the onion, garlic, bay leaves, thyme, salt and pepper. Stir well. At this point you will be horrified – 'Oh no! I've used too many onions!' – but do not fear! Place a lid on the pan. The onions' moisture creates steam and … sure enough, the onion almost melts down, reducing in volume.

Continue to cook like this for about 10 minutes, stirring every few minutes to stop the onions burning or sticking to the base of the pan.

Now, reduce the heat to a gentle simmer and continue to cook – still with the lid on – for 7–8 minutes. Stir once or twice. Pour in the hot water and stir. Next, add the cheese and stir well. Taste and adjust the seasoning accordingly.

If serving with croutons, crumble them into the soup, or serve them with extra grated cheese. Sprinkle over the chives, if using, and ladle the soup from the saucepan at the table.

VARIATIONS

• This soup can be finished by simply adding 100ml double cream or 200ml whole milk at the end.

• For a Normandy-style soup, replace the water with whole milk (or perhaps you'd prefer oat milk).

• For a smooth soup, blend with a stick blender or in a food processor.

• If you want to be classy, dress each bowl of soup with pinches of black onion seeds.

• For a dark onion soup, cook the onions for at least an extra 20 minutes in the pan.

Tomato Soup

PREP 10 MINS / COOK 25 MINS

This rich and deeply satisfying soup is best made in the height of the tomato season. A large amount of fat, ripe tomatoes, with a decent ratio of sweetness to acidity, are mixed with a few cherry tomatoes (these add extra sweetness and colour). For a creamy finish, add a spoonful of crème fraîche or Jersey cream. I like to blend the soup with a moulin-légumes (or food mill), just as my mother did. It's the best gadget for keeping the vibrant red colour of the tomatoes, although a liquidiser will also do the job. The soup can be made a day in advance and refrigerated, or you can freeze it.

SERVES 4–6 (MAKES ABOUT 1.7 LITRES)

½ white onion
3 garlic cloves
1.1kg large, ripe tomatoes (such as Marmande or Coeur de Boeuf)
2 handfuls of cherry tomatoes
1 basil sprig, plus a few leaves to finish
1 sage sprig
3 tablespoons olive oil
1 small rosemary sprig
1 marjoram sprig (optional)
4 tablespoons tomato purée
400ml water
100ml extra-virgin olive oil, plus extra to finish

To finish (optional)
4 tablespoons crème fraîche or Jersey cream
a few handfuls of croutons

TO PREPARE Finely dice the onion and coarsely chop the peeled garlic. Coarsely chop the large tomatoes. Simply remove the stems of the cherry tomatoes, and leave the tomatoes whole. Coarsely chop the basil and sage. Put all of these to one side.

Heat the olive oil in a large saucepan over a medium heat. Add the onion, garlic, sage and rosemary (and marjoram, if using). Cover with a lid and cook for 5 minutes, stirring occasionally.

Add the tomato purée, stir, cover with the lid and continue to cook for 3–4 minutes. Increase the heat to high, add the chopped tomatoes, cherry tomatoes, basil and water. Cover with the lid again and simmer for 15 minutes, stirring occasionally. Remove the pan from the heat and leave to cool.

Pass the liquid through a moulin-légumes or food mill (or purée in a liquidiser) into a clean saucepan. Stir in the extra-virgin olive oil.

At this stage you can either chill the soup and serve it within a couple of days or freeze it. Or serve it straight away, adding the optional garnish – a spoonful of crème fraîche or cream, for richness, and croutons or a drizzle of olive oil and a few basil leaves.

Shellfish and Leek Chowder

PREP 20 MINS / COOK 20 MINS

Chowder. I am intrigued by the apparent French connection to this hearty broth. Going back to the seventeenth and eighteenth centuries, French settlers arrived in what we now know as North America and the Maritime Provinces of Canada. Each settler brought from home a well-used iron pot – a cauldron-like vessel known as *une chaudière*. It is the origin of the word chowder, a true melting pot of cultures. The early recipes called for layers of onion, salt pork and fish, along with biscuits or crackers soaked in milk, with a bottle of red wine – who's complaining? – and more milk. My recipe includes a little pork, milk and wine (but white) and requires mussels, clams and cockles. Today, frozen precooked shellfish is available and can be used in this dish.

SERVES 4

200g clams
200g mussels
200g cockles
1 large Désirée or
  Maris Piper potato
1 large leek
1 onion
1 garlic clove
100g smoked bacon
  (optional)
200ml dry white wine
30g unsalted butter
1 bay leaf
800ml whole milk
grating of fresh root
  ginger (optional)
2 gratings of nutmeg
  (optional)
sea salt flakes and freshly
  ground black pepper
a strong squeeze of
  lemon juice
a handful of roughly
  chopped flat-leaf parsley,
  to garnish (optional)

TO PREPARE Before you start, and if using fresh shellfish, ensure that all the clams, mussels and cockles are tightly closed and not damaged; any that are not should be discarded as they are dead. Wash the shellfish and remove the beards from the mussels. Now prepare the following ingredients, putting them aside as you go. Dice the potato (fingernail size). Halve the leek lengthways, lightly wash away any grit, and finely slice it. Finely slice the onion. Finely slice the peeled garlic clove. If using bacon, slice it finely into thin lardons.

Put a large saucepan on a high heat and give it a moment to pick up some heat. Pour in the white wine and bring it to the boil. Add the shellfish, cover with a lid and cook for 2–3 minutes, until the shells have opened.

Strain into a bowl and leave to cool slightly. Put the cooking liquor to one side, as you'll need it for the soup. Discard any unopened shells. Pick out the clams, mussels and cockles from the opened shells and put them in a bowl with a little cooking liquor poured over them.

In a separate large saucepan on a medium heat, melt the butter and add the potato, leek, onion, garlic and the bay leaf. If using bacon, add this too. Cook for 4–5 minutes – just enough time to soften the onion and leek, not to colour or brown them (stir occasionally to prevent the vegetables from browning).

Add the reserved shellfish cooking liquor, the milk and the ginger and nutmeg, if using, bring to the boil and then reduce to a simmer. Continue to cook for 5–6 minutes. With a stick blender or in a liquidiser, blend to a smooth soup.

Pour the soup into the saucepan and add the clams, mussels and cockles. Reheat over a low–medium heat. Taste and adjust the seasoning with salt, pepper and a strong squeeze of lemon.

Divide the hot chowder into four bowls, scatter with the chopped parsley and serve immediately.

Vegetable and Chervil Soup

PREP 20 MINS / COOK 10–12 MINS

A small tribute to Maman Blanc. And I should say to Papa Blanc, too, as most of the vegetables would come from our garden, which was his great labour of love. The vegetables and herbs can be adapted, according to the season. Chervil is one of my favourite herbs and is very popular in France, but less so in Britain. That's a shame as Britain has the perfect climate for this frost-resistant herb, which is fresh, tangy and slightly parsley-aniseed flavoured. It can be replaced by a tiny bit of tarragon, basil or the fronds of fennel. This soup is cooked in about 10 minutes, and the same method can be used to make thousands of other soups by using only one vegetable, such as courgette, frozen peas or broad beans, or leeks.

SERVES 4–6

1 onion
1 garlic clove
1 medium-sized potato
¼ turnip
½ leek
1 large carrot
½ celery stick
1 courgette
1 ripe tomato
a large handful of chervil
1 tablespoon unsalted butter, plus another to finish (optional)
8 pinches of sea salt
2 pinches of freshly ground white pepper
1.2 litres boiling water
1 tablespoon crème fraîche, to finish

TO PREPARE Finely dice the onion and the peeled garlic. Peel and dice the potato and turnip. Coarsely chop the leek. Peel and chop the carrot into slices. Chop the celery and courgette. Coarsely chop the tomato and the chervil.

In a large saucepan and over a medium heat, soften the onion, garlic and potato in the butter for 3 minutes – this will extract maximum flavour but stir to prevent browning. Season with the salt and white pepper.

Add the turnip, leek, carrot, celery, courgette and tomato. Stir and add the boiling water. Bring to the boil, increase the heat, and cook on a fast boil for 5–7 minutes, until the vegetables are just tender. Stir in the chervil.

To finish the soup, stir in the crème fraîche or butter (or both, if you wish). Taste and correct the seasoning if necessary, then serve. This soup can be puréed in a blender if you prefer a smooth texture.

PISTOU SOUP

Why not try pistou soup, a speciality of the South of France? Make the vegetable and chervil soup using olive oil instead of butter, and then stir in the pistou. To make the pistou: begin by blanching a small bunch of basil (with stalks) in boiling water for 5 seconds, and then plunge the basil into a bowl of iced water; drain and chop. With a blender, purée the basil with 6 tablespoons extra-virgin olive oil, 2 tablespoons water, 1 chopped garlic clove and a tablespoon of grated Parmigiano-Reggiano or Pecorino cheese. Reserve in the fridge for up to a week. Pistou also freezes well.

Easy-peasy Soup

PREP 5 MINS / COOK 10 MINS

This perfectly illustrates how easy it is to prepare a soup for your loved ones. Soup simplicity itself! With just a few ingredients and one vegetable from the freezer, you can make a very tasty, nutritious soup within 15 minutes. Once again, this is a soup that is made without stock. Instead, water is used as a medium. That is how Maman always made her soups, and you can do this too. Serve it hot or, in the summer months, refrigerate the soup and serve it chilled. The mint can be replaced by marjoram, basil or coriander. Once you have made this, you will want to make more soups with other vegetables, be it celery, leeks, carrots or pumpkin …

SERVES 4–5

800ml water
1 garlic clove
2 large mint sprigs
150ml extra-virgin
  olive oil
500g frozen peas
sea salt and black pepper

TO PREPARE First thing, bring the water to the boil in a pan or in your kettle. Boiling water will speed up the cooking time and retain the brightness of the soup, as well as its flavours and most of the nutrients. Finely chop the garlic and coarsely chop the mint leaves.

Heat about a quarter of the olive oil in a large-sized saucepan over a medium heat, add the garlic and sweat it for 1–2 minutes.

Add the peas (still frozen, if you wish) and chopped mint leaves and season with a few pinches of salt and a few turns of pepper. Pour in the boiling water. Bring to the boil for 2–3 minutes.

Turn off the heat and pour in the rest of the extra-virgin olive oil. Then, with a stick blender, purée the soup to the finest consistency.

Taste, taste, taste. Divide the hot pea soup into bowls, and serve.

VARIATIONS

• For a more luxurious soup, you can add a little crème fraîche or yoghurt to the soup – simply stir it in at the end.

• A crusty baguette would be warmly welcomed here.

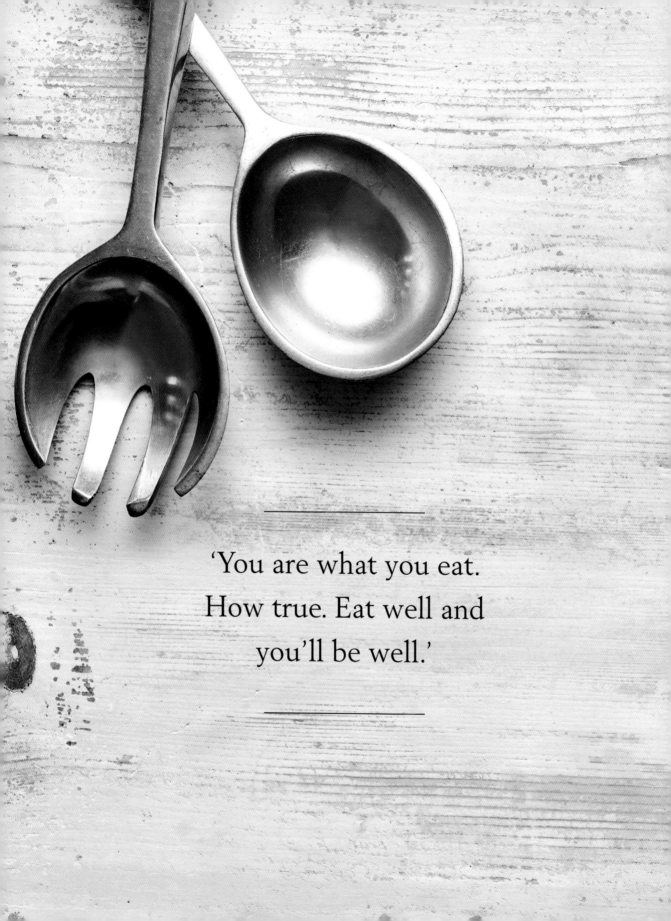

'You are what you eat.
How true. Eat well and
you'll be well.'

SALADS

Beetroot Salad, Hot Smoked
Salmon, Horseradish Crème Fraîche
86

Caesar Salad, Crispy Bacon
89

Pickled Herrings and
Warm Potato Salad
90

Borlotti Bean Salad
93

Courgette Salad
94

Chicory and Orange Salad
97

Salade Niçoise
98

Beetroot Salad, Hot Smoked Salmon, Horseradish Crème Fraîche

PREP 20 MINS / COOK 1–1½ HOURS

Some interesting autumnal flavours and textures are brought together in this simple dish. Please try to buy the best salmon. Organic farmed salmon is more expensive than conventionally farmed salmon, but is certainly worth it, if the budget permits. Other smoked fish, such as smoked mackerel, can be substituted if you prefer. These days there is an exciting selection of beetroot varieties, ranging from ruby and white to yellow and red. These are mostly old varieties that have – or had – been forgotten. The beetroot salad can be prepared up to a few hours in advance of serving, and I like to use an aged balsamic vinegar for this dish, but you may prefer a red wine or white wine vinegar.

SERVES 4

200g hot smoked salmon
sprigs of dill, to garnish
  (optional)

For the beetroot salad
480g baby beetroot
  (mix of ruby, candy
  and golden)
1 small shallot or
  ½ white onion
2 teaspoons balsamic
  vinegar
2 tablespoons extra-
  virgin olive oil
1 tablespoon water
4 pinches of sea salt flakes
4 turns of ground black
  pepper

*For the crème fraîche
dressing*
100g crème fraîche
1 teaspoon horseradish
  sauce (or finely grated
  fresh horseradish)
2 pinches of sea salt flakes
pinch of cayenne pepper
squeeze of lemon juice

TO PREPARE Begin by washing and trimming the beetroot. Place them in a large saucepan and cover with water. Over a high heat, bring to the boil and then reduce to a simmer and cook like this for 1–1½ hours (if you prefer, the beetroot can be steamed). Allow the beetroot to cool slightly before peeling them. Cut them into bite-sized segments and place them in a bowl. Pull the skin off the hot smoked salmon and break the fish into bite-sized pieces. Finely chop the shallot and add to the bowl.

Add the balsamic vinegar, extra-virgin olive oil, water, salt and pepper to the bowl and toss the ingredients together. Taste and adjust the seasoning, if necessary.

Now make the crème fraîche dressing. In a bowl, simply combine the crème fraîche, horseradish sauce, salt, cayenne pepper and add a squeeze of lemon juice. Taste and adjust the seasoning as required.

Arrange the beetroot salad in the centre of a serving plate, top with the pieces of hot smoked salmon and spoon crème fraîche dressing over or around. Garnish with a few sprigs of dill, if using, before serving.

Caesar Salad, Crispy Bacon

PREP 5 MINS / COOK 10 MINS

As with so many of the classics, there's a delightfully charming tale behind Caesar Salad. Let me take you back to America's Prohibition era of the 1920s … thirsty Californians crossed the nearby border to drink – and occasionally eat – in the Mexican town of Tijuana. There, a restaurant called Caesar's Place became hugely popular. Everyone liked the charismatic Italian-American owner, Cesare Cardini, but they fell in love with the salad that he served. I am sorry to tell you it is not named after an emperor, but my God, it is definitely a dish fit for one – crunchy, crisp, fresh and bursting with full-on flavours. Here's my take on the salad. Try the dressing as a dip with crisps or slices of raw celery and carrots.

SERVES 4 AS A LIGHT LUNCH, SNACK OR STARTER

2 romaine (also known as cos) lettuces

8 slices of smoked streaky bacon (or 200g bacon lardons)

2 tablespoons olive oil

For the Caesar dressing

1 garlic clove

15g Parmigiano-Reggiano cheese, plus extra to finish

6 anchovy fillets, in oil, plus extra to finish

2 teaspoons white wine vinegar

5 tablespoons Mayonnaise or Chickpea Mayonnaise (shop-bought or see pages 111 and 63)

few turns of ground black pepper

To finish

1 tarragon sprig

4 flat-leaf parsley sprigs

TO PREPARE Chop away the woody base of the lettuces, but keep the lettuces whole and intact. Now slice the lettuces into quarters and put these to one side. Dice the bacon into pieces of about 2cm. Coarsely chop the peeled garlic and grate the cheese.

Begin by making the dressing. Blend all the dressing ingredients in a food processor or using a stick blender to create a smooth sauce. Put the dressing to one side or refrigerate until required (you can make it 1–2 days in advance).

Heat the oil in a large non-stick frying pan on a medium–high heat. Add the bacon pieces and sauté for 4–5 minutes, or until they are golden and slightly crisp. Use a slotted spoon to remove the bacon and lay it on kitchen paper, leaving the fat in the pan.

Return the pan to a medium heat, lay the lettuce quarters in the hot pan, cut-side down, and pan-fry them, without turning, for 2–3 minutes, until the leaves are golden brown on one side. Turn and brown the other cut side. Remove the pan from the heat.

Caesar Salad is at its most imperial when served in a shallow bowl or dish. Arrange the lettuce halves, coloured side up, in the bowl. Spoon the crispy bacon over the lettuce and spoon the dressing over the bacon. Finely chop the tarragon and coarsely chop the parsley, combine the two herbs on the chopping board and then sprinkle them over the salad. Sprinkle with shavings of Parmigiano and add a few whole anchovy fillets. Serve.

Pickled Herrings and Warm Potato Salad

PREP 5 MINS / COOK 20 MINS

Among the many culinary skills of my British friends, pickling is certainly one of them. Here is a fine example of a pleasing dish where the humble herring, once pickled, becomes a nation's favourite. Taste, and you will also notice how potatoes absorb all the flavours of a dressing if they are mixed when the potatoes are still quite hot.

SERVES 4

600g new potatoes
1 tarragon sprig
½ red onion
2 bay leaves
8 pickled herrings/
    rollmops
3 tablespoons extra-
    virgin olive oil
sea salt and black pepper

To garnish
a handful of finely
    chopped chives
2 handfuls of watercress
    (optional)

TO PREPARE Quarter the new potatoes. Pick the tarragon leaves from the sprig and finely chop. Finely slice the red onion.

Cook the potatoes with the bay leaves in a large saucepan of gently boiling, salted water. They'll take 15–20 minutes. Check they're done by inserting the tip of a knife into the largest potato. Even better, taste!

As the potatoes bubble, drain the herrings into a bowl, keeping the pickling liquor as you'll need it for the dressing.

Pour the olive oil into a bowl with the pickling liquor and stir. Taste and adjust with more oil, to your liking.

Now, drain the potatoes, let the steam leave them and while they are still hot, transfer them to a serving bowl. Pour over the olive oil-pickling liquor mixture.

Add the onion and tarragon, season with salt and pepper, and toss the salad – but carefully, please, so as not to break the potatoes.

Taste to check the seasoning and adjust accordingly. Garnish with the chopped chives and top with the pickled herrings and watercress, if using. Spoon over any remaining dressing and serve the salad while it is warm.

Borlotti Bean Salad

PREP 5 MINS

Here's a salad that takes just a few minutes to make. It will take longer if you wish to cook the borlotti beans (if you do so, please see page 294). But if you use good-quality tinned borlotti beans, then searching for the tin opener will be the most time-consuming part of creating this dish. Instead of borlotti, why not try other varieties of beans, such as cannellini, flageolet, haricot or kidney? Your favourite spices, herbs or lettuce leaves, such as rocket, would be a lovely addition to this salad.

SERVES 4–6

2 tins (each 400g)
   borlotti beans or
   cooked beans (see
   page 294)
2 large ripe tomatoes or
   10–15 cherry tomatoes
½ red chilli
½ handful of coarsely
   chopped flat-leaf parsley
¼ handful of coarsely
   chopped garlic chives
   (optional)
1 garlic clove
sea salt
3 turns of ground
   black pepper
3 tablespoons extra-
   virgin olive oil
2 tablespoons red or
   white wine vinegar

TO PREPARE Have to hand a chopping board, sharp knife for chopping and a serving bowl. Drain the beans and rinse them for a few seconds under cold running water. Leave them to drain while getting on with the other bits. Chop the tomatoes into quarters or halves and finely slice the chilli.

Transfer the tomatoes, chilli, parsley and garlic chives, if using, to the bowl. Finely slice the peeled garlic clove, add a little salt, and then crush it with the back of a kitchen knife to turn it to a paste (or simply use a garlic crusher). Add the garlic and the beans to the bowl. Add a generous pinch of salt, the pepper, extra-virgin oil and vinegar. Toss the salad. Before serving, taste and, if required, adjust the seasoning.

Courgette Salad

PREP 10 MINS

Spring meets summer in this quick and easy salad, with elegant flavours and textures. It's a wonderful fresh, crunchy, tasty starter or the perfect accompaniment to grilled meats or fish, such as the Spicy Chicken Paillard on page 155.

SERVES 2 AS A MAIN DISH OR 4 AS A SIDE

4 courgettes
2 garlic cloves
a handful of basil leaves
6 pinches of sea salt flakes
8 turns of ground black pepper
8 tablespoons extra-virgin olive oil
4 tablespoons white wine vinegar (or lemon juice)
80g crumbled feta cheese
a generous handful of rocket leaves

TO PREPARE To cook this dish … What am I saying? There is no cooking! This salad is simply a case of preparation. Slice the courgettes lengthways into thin strips. To do this, you could use a potato peeler or kitchen knife. A mandolin is best for the job – the slicer rather than musical instrument – but please use a finger guard. And for those who love gadgets, there's the spiralizer. Anyway, the strips should be about 2–3mm thick. Transfer the courgette slices to a bowl. Finely slice the peeled garlic and add it to the same bowl. Tear the basil leaves and, again, they go into the same bowl. You are moments from completion.

Add the salt, pepper, oil and vinegar. Toss the salad and leave it for about 5 minutes, enabling a perfect exchange of flavours. Notice how the courgette slices soften while they marinate (this salad can be prepared and then refrigerated up to 30 minutes before serving).

Taste. Adjust the seasoning accordingly and, if necessary, add a little more oil or vinegar to your taste. Just before serving, add the feta and rocket leaves. Toss the salad well so that the leaves are coated and serve from the bowl. And there you have it – a delicious 10-minute salad!

VARIATIONS

• There are many ways of elegantly dressing up this salad: sprinkle with grated Parmigiano instead of the feta or slivers of sun-dried tomatoes. Or how about chilli flakes or chilli oil?

• You can also flash the salad under a hot grill before serving, or toss in a pan over a high flame for a few seconds, and serve it warm.

Chicory and Orange Salad

PREP 10 MINS

When the autumn chill sets in, here's a salad to lift the spirits. The red or purple chicory tends to be a bit more expensive than the white, but it's good for your health and looks lovely and festive. Please add to this salad as you wish: little croutons, crumbled goat's cheese, coarsely chopped celery leaves, nuts and seeds. Some crunchy kale or watercress leaves wouldn't go amiss, or fine slices of apple or pear. Or enjoy with a sourdough loaf.

SERVES 4–6

3 oranges
3 heads of yellow chicory
3 heads of red chicory
½ red onion
2 handfuls of walnuts
a handful of pistachios
 (optional)
6 tablespoons walnut oil
4 pinches of sea salt
5–6 turns of ground
 black pepper

TO PREPARE With a sharp knife, remove the skin from 1 orange. Slice the orange, crossways, at intervals of about 1cm, then dice each slice. Put these to one side. Squeeze the juice from the two remaining oranges and put the juice to one side. Trim the bottom off the chicory heads and trim the base of the leaves that come away. Halve each chicory lengthways, and then chop each half into three pieces lengthways through the root. Slice the red onion as finely as possible.

Transfer the diced orange and chicory pieces to a serving bowl along with the red onion.

Coarsely crush the walnuts (and pistachios, if using) between two pieces of baking parchment. Now pour the crushed nuts from the paper into the bowl – I'm trying to save on the washing-up.

OK, let's make the dressing … Pour the orange juice and walnut oil into a bowl (or jug). Add the salt and pepper. Stir, taste and adjust the seasoning if necessary. The dressing can sit for about an hour, but stir it every now and again, and then just before it is poured over the salad.

Pour the dressing over the salad, toss the salad well and serve from the bowl. Alternatively, arrange the chicory leaves in a shallow dish, sprinkle over the crushed nuts and drizzle with the dressing.

Salade Niçoise

PREP 10 MINS / COOK 15 MINS

I used to dream of living beside the Mediterranean in the South of France. Then I was fortunate enough to realise that dream, and today I have a little place that is just minutes away from Nice. With its seductive scents of herbs, lavender, sea and pine, and the lazy sounds of the crickets, here is the town that gave its name to this great, colourful classic. Salade Niçoise is *une grand dame*, who, over the years, has seen off all the salad trends. In the summer and early autumn serve it as a starter or main course, and don't forget to chill the Provence rosé. I call it Heaven.

SERVES 4–6

½ red onion
4 big, fat tomatoes
  or a handful of
  cherry tomatoes
½ small cucumber
1 red or green pepper
2 baby gem lettuces
4 handfuls of radicchio
  (or mixed salad leaves)
100g French beans
4 medium eggs
  (preferably organic
  or free-range)
a handful of basil leaves

For the dressing
1 garlic clove
6 tablespoons extra-
  virgin olive oil
2 tablespoons red wine
  vinegar or white
  balsamic vinegar
6 pinches of sea salt flakes
8 turns of ground black
  pepper

To finish
300g good-quality tinned/
  jarred tuna
12–16 anchovy fillets, in oil
100g black olives, pitted
  (or little Niçoise olives,
  if you are a purist)

TO PREPARE First, put some lightly salted water on to boil in a medium-sized pan for the beans, and prepare the following ingredients, placing them into a large bowl as you go and loosely tossing together:

Red onion: chop it.

Tomatoes: quarter them or chop into chunks (or in half if using cherry tomatoes).

Cucumber: halve it lengthways, remove the seeds, and then roughly slice.

Red or green pepper: halve it lengthways, deseed the pepper and finely slice.

Baby gem lettuce: slice it into quarters, lengthways.

Radicchio (or mixed salad leaves): coarsely chop or tear. If using baby salad leaves, these can stay whole.

Garlic: peel and finely slice (reserve for the dressing).

Cook the beans for 5 minutes in the boiling water. Use a slotted spoon to remove from the water and place them in a bowl of cold water. Keep the hot water in the saucepan. Return the pan to the heat, bring the water to a gentle boil, and use a spoon to slide the eggs into the water. Cook them for 10 minutes.

Cool the eggs in cold water for 1 minute, then remove the shell while the eggs are still warm – the steam between the shell and the egg white makes an easy job of peeling. Set aside the peeled eggs in a bowl of cold water.

Halve the eggs, and put them on a plate to one side. *Voilà!* Now, the dressing …

Add the garlic, olive oil, vinegar, salt and pepper to a bowl and whisk to emulsify. Adjust the seasoning accordingly. Pour the dressing over the salad.

Add the basil leaves to the bowl and gently toss the salad, ready to serve it from the bowl or arrange it on a serving dish. Before serving, garnish with the tuna, egg halves, anchovies and that other essential taste of Nice – the black olives.

My love for
SALADS

Salad is the simplest form of gastronomy. A few chopped vegetables combined with a dressing and some fresh herbs. What could be easier? However, it is worth giving a bit of thought to a salad. Begin with the best ingredients, and then you are almost there: Mother Nature has done all the hard work. Every day in my childhood home, we'd have a bowl of salad leaves, served with a tray of four or five cheeses. Looking at the salad bowl, you knew which season you were in. There was frisée and romaine in the spring. In the summer, we ate Reine des Glaces (Queen of the Ices) and in the autumn and winter months, mâche (lamb's tongue), as well as radicchio.

I remember a special salad moment in the 1980s. I was at Jamin, Joël Robuchon's restaurant in Paris, and was served a dish of golden, deep-fried shavings of parsnip and sweet potato with garden leaves and fresh herbs, which included dill, peppermint, tarragon, chervil, coriander and marjoram. It was absolutely fantastic. And when they are done well – and again, with good-quality ingredients – who can resist the classics, from Caesar to Niçoise and Waldorf, and salads of potato, chicken, tuna? A great salad should combine sweetness with acidity and have a texture with decent crunch.

Salad, the word itself, originates from *salata*, the Latin for salted, and stems from the Ancient Romans' custom of dipping lettuce leaves in salt or brine before eating them. In 2012, I embarked on a major lettuce challenge with the wonderful Anna Greenland, who was head vegetable gardener at Le Manoir. We trialled four dozen varieties of salad leaves and I would like to share with you our soil-speckled notes in case you'd like to grow them at home. I loved the crispiness of the Corbana cos variety, and two baby-leaf varieties, Oaking and Redza. We liked a butterhead called Descartes, a crinkly Batavia called Maritima, and a romaine variety, Rubens Red. From those trials, and still today, my favourite lettuce is a variety that was grown in Maman Blanc's garden at Le Manoir. The Reine des Glaces is a crisphead variety and she is suitably named: the colder the weather, the sweeter and crunchier she becomes.

Morteau Sausage Salad with Poached Egg

PREP 5 MINS / COOK 45 MINS, BUT LITTLE EFFORT

SERVES 4

1 Morteau sausage
2 tablespoons white
   wine vinegar
4 medium eggs (preferably
   organic or free-range)
   (optional)
2 pinches of sea salt
pinch of ground
   black pepper

*Dijon mustard dressing
(optional)*
1 tablespoon Dijon mustard
3 tablespoons extra-virgin
   olive oil
1½ tablespoons white
   wine vinegar
2 tablespoons warm water
2 pinches of sea salt flakes

For the white wine potatoes
500g Belle de Fontenay
   potatoes (or Charlotte)
1 small shallot (about 50g)
45ml white wine vinegar
2 tablespoons dry
   white wine
3 bay leaves
1 teaspoon sea salt flakes
pinch of ground white
   pepper
45ml vegetable oil

To finish
100g salad leaves, such as
   frisée, treviso, chicory or
   mixed salad leaves
a handful of finely
   chopped chives

This salad represents the heart and values of Franche-Comté, and really demonstrates the region's gastronomy. It is an alluring tapestry of huge pine forests and fields, where cows graze cheerfully. These cows provide the whey of the milk. The farmer's pigs, in turn, are fattened on the whey. When the pig is fat and ready, it is the pine that is used to smoke the pork sausage. *Voilà!* There you have *saucisse de Morteau*, the world-beating sausage. It's all local.

TO PREPARE Wash the potatoes; no need to peel them. Finely chop the shallot.

Make the mustard dressing first … In a medium bowl, whisk the Dijon mustard, oil, vinegar, water and salt. Place the salad leaves on top of the dressing, ready to toss through at the last minute before serving.

Prick the sausage with a fork. Place it in a large pan of cold water and bring to a simmer. Add the potatoes and continue to simmer for 20 minutes. With a slotted spoon, remove the potatoes from the water and leave them to cool slightly before cutting them into slices, about 1cm thick.

Meanwhile, leave the sausage in the pan of hot water for a further 20 minutes. It will continue to cook in the residual heat.

Transfer the shallot to a small saucepan and add the white wine vinegar, white wine, bay leaves, salt and pepper. Bring to the boil and let it boil for 10 seconds before removing the pan from the heat. Pour in the vegetable oil. Pour this hot dressing over the warm potatoes, but keep about a tablespoon of the dressing to dress the salad leaves just before you are ready to serve.

If you are feeling in the mood to serve my beloved Morteau with poached eggs, cook them like this … In a large saucepan on a medium heat, bring about 2 litres of water to a simmer and add the white wine vinegar. Crack each egg into a ramekin (or cup). Place a ramekin at the very edge of the water and gently slide an egg into the water. Do the same with the remaining three eggs. The eggs will take 3–4 minutes to poach.

Remove the eggs from the water with a slotted spoon and place them on kitchen paper to absorb the excess water on the white. (I like to take a pair of kitchen scissors and trim away the untidy white strands.) Season.

Cut the sausage into thin slices and arrange on the plates or a large serving dish with the potatoes. Top with the dressed salad leaves. Finish with the poached eggs, if using, scatter with the chives and serve.

Tomato Salad, Maman Blanc

PREP 10 MINS / MARINATE AT LEAST 5 MINS

This salad is very Maman Blanc in style, but I have added something – mozzarella – which is not very Maman Blanc, at all. We did not have mozzarella in Franche-Comté, where I was my father's helper in his garden, assisting with the planting of tomatoes, and then nurturing them until they were plump and ready to be picked. Although often they were picked when slightly under-ripe before they could fall to the ground and bruise. Then they were left to ripen on a kitchen window sill, finished by the warmth of sunbeams. Of course, the better the tomato, the better the salad. My favourite mozzarella comes from Laverstoke Park Farm in Hampshire, where my friend Jody Scheckter, the world champion racing driver turned farmer, keeps a herd of buffalo.

SERVES 4

1.2kg heirloom tomatoes
(Tiger-striped, plum,
Black Russian, etc)

½ red onion

1 garlic clove

2 pinches of sea salt flakes

6 turns of ground
black pepper

2 tablespoons white
wine vinegar

4 tablespoons extra-
virgin olive oil

2 balls of mozzarella
cheese

4 basil sprigs

TO PREPARE Slice all the tomatoes into bite-sized wedges and place them in a large bowl. Finely slice the onion and add to the same bowl. Crush the peeled garlic clove with the back of a knife, finely slice it and then add it to the bowl.

Season the salad with the salt and pepper and add the white wine vinegar and olive oil. Toss the salad, and leave it for at least 5 minutes to marinate – enough time for an exchange of flavours.

Arrange the tomato salad on a large serving dish. Cut the mozzarella balls into quarters and place them around the salad with the basil sprigs. Serve.

VARIATION

Add a few handfuls of pitted Kalamata olives. These can be dried for 1 hour in an oven preheated to 100°C/80°C fan/gas ¼ and then finely chopped and scattered over the salad.

Vegetable Escabeche

PREP 25 MINS / MARINATE OVERNIGHT

A spicy and chilled marinade originating from Spain and the South of France, escabeche is a technique of preserving meat, fish and vegetables. It is also refreshing, flavoursome and this recipe is full of contrasting textures. As it requires at least 12 hours to marinate, it's a good idea to prepare it a day in advance. You can serve this as a summer salad or as an accompaniment to Seared Sesame Tuna (see page 131), pan-fried salmon, stir-fried prawns or a ceviche of scallops. Pickled ginger and finely chopped lemongrass may be added to the escabeche, which is an expression of summer's bounty.

SERVES 4

½ mooli (daikon) radish
I carrot
2 breakfast radishes
¼ fennel bulb
I courgette
I shallot
I garlic clove
I basil sprig
3 kaffir lime leaves
   (optional)
3 tablespoons extra-
   virgin olive oil
juice of 2 oranges
juice of ½ lemon
3 pinches of sea salt flakes
3 pinches of caster sugar
2 pinches of cayenne
   pepper

To finish
a handful of coarsely
   chopped coriander
   leaves
2 tablespoons extra-
   virgin olive oil

TO PREPARE Peel the mooli and carrot. Use a mandolin slicer or very sharp knife to finely slice the mooli and carrot widthways and the radishes, fennel and courgette lengthways. Transfer them to a bowl. Finely slice the shallot widthways and add it to the mix. Prepare the other ingredients, adding them to the bowl of prepared vegetables as you go … Finely chop and crush the peeled garlic with the back of a knife. Tear the basil. If using the lime leaves, finely chop them.

Add the olive oil and the juice of the oranges and lemon half to the bowl. Add the sea salt, caster sugar and cayenne pepper. Mix well, cover and refrigerate for at least 12 hours (preferably overnight).

To finish the dish, mix the coriander with the escabeche. Serve the escabeche in a large serving bowl or dish, or as individual portions. Just before serving, treat the escabeche to a dash or two of your finest extra-virgin olive oil.

Crab Salad with Pink Grapefruit

PREP 20 MINS

Shellfish and citrus have enjoyed one of the longest-lasting marriages in food history. Since ancient times they have been together, the most harmonious pairing on the palate. Think of the flavours of lobster, crayfish, mussels and prawns and how they are heightened dramatically simply by a squeeze of lemon. Here it is pink grapefruit that adds its own sweet-sour qualities to the crabmeat, lifting the flavours. What of the budget? True, crab is quite pricey but, as a treat, this is a wonderful starter or light, healthy lunch.

SERVES 2

1 pink grapefruit
mesclun salad leaves,
   to serve

For the crab salad
¼ bunch of coriander
125g white crabmeat
35g natural yoghurt
2 pinches of sea salt flakes
pinch of cayenne pepper
zest and juice of ½ lime

*For the brown crab
mayonnaise (the liquids
are in grams, as it's easier
to weigh on scales)*
75g brown crabmeat
20g lemon juice
10g Dijon mustard
2 pinches of sea salt flakes
½ pinch of cayenne
   pepper
70g sunflower oil
20g extra-virgin olive oil

TO PREPARE Slice the grapefruit into segments and arrange them on a plate. Finely chop the coriander.

For the crab salad, place the white crabmeat, yoghurt, sea salt flakes and cayenne pepper in a bowl. Add the zest and juice of the lime half and the coriander. Mix, taste and adjust the seasoning if necessary. Cover and keep in the fridge until required.

For the brown crab mayonnaise, in a food processor (or in a bowl, and with a stick blender), blend the brown crabmeat, lemon juice, mustard, salt and cayenne pepper to create a smooth purée.

In a jug, combine the sunflower oil and extra-virgin olive oil. Now, make the mayonnaise ... With the processor on medium speed, pour the oils into the crabmeat mixture in a steady trickle to create a thick, smooth emulsion. Taste and correct the seasoning. Place in a bowl, cover and refrigerate until required.

Serve the grapefruit alongside the crab salad in one bowl, the brown crab mayonnaise in another bowl and the salad leaves in a final bowl.

Celeriac Remoulade

PREP 20 MINS

Shop-bought mayonnaise is in most fridges in the land, and I am not on a mission to change that. However, I'd gently urge you, please, to make your own mayonnaise every now and again. This silky, creamy sauce is versatile, and can be whipped up in moments. For a vegan version, try the Chickpea Mayonnaise (see page 63) in which egg yolk is replaced with chickpea water. From mayonnaise, you can make many other sauces, including aioli (by adding crushed garlic). Or you can create this celeriac remoulade, served with a garnish of chicory leaves and walnuts in a walnut oil dressing. The remoulade will keep in the fridge for up to two days.

SERVES 4

350g celeriac
1 Granny Smith apple

For the mayonnaise
2 medium egg yolks
   (preferably organic
   or free-range)
1 teaspoon Dijon mustard
150ml groundnut oil
   (or vegetable or
   sunflower oil)
1 teaspoon white
   wine vinegar
pinch of sea salt flakes
pinch of cayenne pepper
1 teaspoon lemon juice

For the salad garnish
40g walnuts
8 yellow or red
   chicory leaves
10ml walnut oil
10ml white wine
   vinegar
½ bunch of finely
   chopped chives

TO PREPARE Peel and finely slice or coarsely grate the celeriac into long strips, using a mandolin or spiralizer if you have one. Finely grate the apple. Coarsely chop the walnuts.

In a large bowl, whisk together the egg yolks and mustard until fully incorporated. Continuing to whisk, slowly add the oil in a steady trickle and you'll see how it thickens. Next, whisk in the vinegar, salt, cayenne pepper and lemon juice. Taste, and adjust the seasoning accordingly. Add the celeriac and apple to the mayonnaise.

For the salad garnish, place the chicory leaves in a bowl, add the walnut oil and vinegar and toss the salad.

Arrange the dressed chicory leaves on a large platter and top with the celeriac remoulade. Scatter the walnuts and chives over the dish.

VARIATION

For an extra garnish to wow your guests, use a sharp knife to cut four fine slices from one side of the apple before you grate it, and cut into matchsticks. Add 1 teaspoon of lemon juice to the apple and scatter over the salad just before serving.

My love for
CELERIAC

To many, it is an ugly, knobbly, misshapen vegetable. But to me, the celeriac has always been a thing of great beauty and is one of my favourite winter vegetables. As a child, I liked to eat it raw. I beg you to grate it, and try it raw with a light coating of walnut or hazelnut oil or a good mayonnaise. My mother would often make sauerkraut, replacing the traditional cabbage with sliced celeriac.

Well, over time my love for celeriac has not faded one little bit. And for me, celeriac unites the garden of my childhood with the garden of my adult life. In the chillier months, I like to stroll through the potager at Le Manoir, conducting an early-morning inspection of the rows and rows of celeriac. They line the soil like a regiment of green-topped root vegetables, getting fatter with each passing day. The celeriac's enemies are everywhere, whether it's flies or other insects. And celeriac's old enemy is time: little by little, it is nibbled by the creatures of the underground world. Life, you see, certainly goes on under the soil, even if we cannot see it.

Now, don't throw away that green top – it helps to make the tastiest soup for two people. Dice two potatoes and brown them in a knob of sizzling butter. Then add the chopped celeriac tops, and pour in 500ml boiling water. Cook on a full boil for 10 minutes. Blend to a purée, taste and season. For a celeriac purée, cook diced celeriac in butter, and then add milk; cook it slowly, slowly and then blend. If you are fortunate enough to have black truffle, a few shavings of it over the celeriac can only heighten the eating experience.

'Music while cooking?
Depending on the
mood, I love to listen
to romantic classical,
soothing chill or the
hardest rock 'n' roll.'

FISH DISHES

Mussels:

Moules Marinière

137

Mussels with Lemongrass,
Lime and Coconut

137

Moules Provençal

140

Pan-fried Fillet of Salmon,
Chive-butter Sauce and
Wilted Spinach

143

Flash-fried Squid, Fennel
and Rocket Salad

144

My Love for Fennel

146

Pan-fried Slip Sole

149

Cod 'Cassoulet'

PREP 5 MINS / COOK 15 MINS

A quick one-pan meal, this cassoulet is wholesome, full of flavour and freshness, with a touch of spicy heat. I know, I know, it is cassoulet with fish, and not the traditional cassoulet of southwest France, which is made with half a pig. It really doesn't need an accompaniment, but can be served with a salad or a side dish of wilted greens and a spelt loaf to help mop up the sauce, French-style.

SERVES 2

2 cod fillets (each approx.
  140g), skinless
4 large pinches of sea
  salt flakes
4 turns of ground
  black pepper
½ white onion
100g chorizo
1 tin (400g) mixed beans
6 tablespoons olive oil
400g tomato passata
generous pinch of
  cayenne pepper
2 heaped teaspoons
  smoked paprika
  (optional)

To finish
juice of ½ lemon
extra-virgin olive oil
a small handful of
  chopped flat-leaf
  parsley

TO PREPARE Season each cod fillet with 2 pinches of sea salt and a couple of turns of black pepper and set aside. Finely dice the onion and then dice the chorizo. Drain and lightly rinse the mixed beans.

Heat the oil in a large non-stick sauté pan (or deep-sided frying pan) on a medium–high heat. Add the onion, chorizo and remaining salt and pepper, cover with a lid and cook for 3–4 minutes, stirring occasionally to prevent burning.

Add the mixed beans, passata, cayenne pepper and paprika, if using. Stir and cook – still over a medium–high heat, but without a lid on the pan – for a further 3–4 minutes, stirring occasionally.

Reduce the heat to medium and lay the cod fillets in the pan. They should be semi-immersed in the cassoulet but, if not, just add a little water. Cover with the lid and reduce the heat so that the cassoulet simmers gently for 5–6 minutes. The cod fillets do not need to be turned.

Remove the pan from the heat, add the lemon juice, a couple of dashes of extra-virgin olive oil and scatter with the chopped parsley. Serve from the pan, at the table.

VARIATIONS

• The virtue of cassoulet is that it can be made with a wide variety of vegetables, pulses and spices. The mixed beans in this recipe can be substituted with your favourite lentils. You may wish to include aubergine or stir in slices of roasted red peppers towards the end of cooking.

• Substitute the cayenne pepper with any of these: peri peri, chilli powder, Espelette pepper or ½ finely sliced red or green chilli.

• If you wish, replace the cod with fillets of haddock, pollock or salmon.

Pan-fried Cod, Brown Shrimp Sauce, with Peas and Spinach

PREP 5 MINS / COOK 10 MINS

This fish dish, made within 15 minutes, is hugely flavoursome, luxurious and rich. It is also a very pleasant way to learn the technique of pan-frying. True, there's quite a bit of butter, which doesn't quite correspond to my profile, but it's still yummy once in a while. Also, I urge you please to try this technique of cooking the peas and spinach, the side dish in my recipe. It really is the best way to maximise taste, texture and flavour, while retaining all the nutrients of the vegetables. Plus, it can be prepared in advance and then cooked as the main dish is almost ready to be served. So very, very simple!

SERVES 4

4 cod fillets (each approx. 140g), skin on
4 pinches of sea salt flakes
4 turns of ground black pepper
2 tablespoons unsalted butter
2 tablespoons water
2 x 50g pots of potted brown shrimp
juice of 1 small lemon
4 chopped flat-leaf parsley sprigs (optional)

For the peas and spinach
½ teaspoon unsalted butter
2 tablespoons water
200g peas
200g spinach
2 pinches of sea salt flakes
4 turns of ground black pepper

VARIATIONS

Add chopped capers, gherkins and shallots to the brown shrimp sauce for extra flavour, texture and acidity.

First, prepare the peas and spinach. Put the butter, water and peas in a medium-sized saucepan or sauté pan. Place the spinach on top and season with the sea salt and pepper. Cover with a lid. Reserve until needed.

Now to the fish … You'll need a sauté or frying pan that's large enough for the cod fillets (about 25cm to 30cm).

Season the cod fillets with the sea salt and pepper. Melt the butter in the pan on a medium heat. As the butter foams, turns golden and smells nutty, that's the moment to lay the cod fillets into the pan, skin-side down. Pan-fry them for 5 minutes. It should be a gentle sizzle – simply reduce the heat if it seems too high (if the heat is too fierce, the butter will burn).

Start to cook the peas and spinach – with a lid on the pan – on a medium–high heat. They will be ready in 4 minutes.

Turn the cod fillets in the pan and fry them for a further 4–5 minutes. Remove the pan from the heat, transfer the cod fillets to a dish and keep them in a warm part of the kitchen.

Return the pan to the heat, add the water and the brown shrimp with its butter. Bring this quickly to the boil and when it steams, add the juice of the lemon. Scatter with the parsley, if using.

Serve from the pan at the table, placing a fillet on each plate and a spoonful of peas and spinach. Finish with a generous spoonful – or two – of shrimps and buttery lemon sauce.

Curried Crab

PREP 5 MINS / COOK 12 MINS

A mildly spicy dish, this is easily prepared, swiftly cooked and on the table within 20 minutes, start to finish. Crab and curry leaves make the perfect marriage (as much as any marriage can be perfect). Coconut milk adds creamy richness, while tamarind is unmistakably tangy. Curried Crab can be eaten on its own or accompanied by Boiled Rice (see page 292).

SERVES 4

2 white onions
3 garlic cloves
2cm piece of fresh
   root ginger
1 red or green chilli
2 tablespoons rapeseed
   oil (or sunflower or
   vegetable oil)
about a dozen curry leaves
150g sugar snap peas
   (or mangetout)
1 teaspoon ground
   coriander
1 teaspoon ground
   turmeric
3 pinches of sea salt flakes
1 tin (400ml) coconut milk
60g tamarind paste
300g crabmeat (mixture
   of white and brown)

To finish
a handful of coarsely
   chopped coriander
½ lemon, for squeezing

TO PREPARE This curry is very quick – and enjoyable – to make, and it is best to have all the ingredients prepared before the pan meets the heat. Halve and finely slice the onions lengthways. Finely slice the peeled garlic and ginger. Coarsely chop the chilli. Put all of these to one side.

Heat the oil in a large sauté or deep-sided frying pan on a high heat. Add the chilli and sauté it in the hot oil for about 30 seconds. Add the curry leaves, stir, and fry them, again for about 30 seconds.

Add the onion and sugar snap peas (or mangetout), stir and continue to fry for 3–4 minutes until the onion has softened and is lightly golden. Stir in the ground coriander, turmeric, garlic, ginger and salt and sauté for a further 2–3 minutes.

Now, pour in the coconut milk and reduce the heat to low–medium. Add the tamarind paste and crabmeat and stir. Simmer gently for 2–3 minutes – see how the coconut milk reduces and becomes thick and velvety.

Finally, stir in the chopped coriander, add a few squeezes of lemon and remove the pan from the heat. Taste and, if necessary, adjust the seasoning with salt and lemon juice, and serve from the pan at the table.

VARIATIONS

• The sugar snap peas (or mangetout) can be replaced, of course. Try spinach or peas, adding them towards the end of cooking. Or Swiss chard, dicing the stalks to about 1cm and roughly chopping the leaves.

• In the winter months, diced Jerusalem artichokes add a pleasant taste and texture.

Grilled Sardines and Warm Tomato Salad

PREP 5 MINS / COOK 5 MINS

The waters around Cornwall are rich in sardines, and this is a lovely dish that celebrates the humble little fish. A tomato salad is placed on a baking tray, and the sardines are placed on top. You may prefer butterflied sardines, which your fishmonger can prepare for you. These small, tasty fish require no more than 5 minutes under a high grill. You may wish to serve it with a crusty baguette, the perfect sponge for the juices in the baking tray. A glass of rosé or crisp, dry white wine will not feel out of place.

SERVES 4 AS A STARTER OR 2 AS A MAIN COURSE

8 sardines

For the salad
4 big, fat, ripe heritage
  or mixed coloured
  tomatoes
2 garlic cloves
½ red onion
2 basil sprigs
1 tablespoon white
  wine vinegar
4 tablespoons extra-
  virgin olive oil
3 thyme sprigs
1 rosemary sprig
sea salt flakes and ground
  black pepper

To finish
extra-virgin olive oil
½ lemon

TO PREPARE Coarsely chop the tomatoes – keeping them quite chunky – and place them in a large bowl. Finely slice the peeled garlic cloves and add them to the bowl. Finely slice the red onion and, yes, in it goes. Coarsely chop the basil.

Pour the white wine vinegar and extra-virgin olive oil into the bowl. Add the basil and the thyme and rosemary sprigs. Season with 3 pinches of sea salt flakes and 6 turns of black pepper. Gently toss the salad.

Preheat the grill to high.

Spread the tomato salad onto a large baking tray. Lay the sardines on top of the salad. Over each sardine sprinkle a pinch of salt and a turn or two of black pepper.

Grill for 4–5 minutes, until the sardines are blistered and golden and the tomatoes are hot but barely cooked. Finally, finish with a dash or two of extra-virgin olive oil and a few squeezes of lemon juice.

Serve from the baking tray in the middle of your table, taking care as the dish will be hot. I wish I was there with you – this is such a fabulous, aromatic cocktail of herbs, earth and sea.

VARIATION

The sardines can be substituted with 4 small mackerel fillets. They will require 6–7 minutes under the grill.

My love for
TOMATOES

What a joy to enter the large greenhouse at Le Manoir and to be greeted by a forest of towering tomato vines and an abundance of extraordinary colours, different shapes, sizes. As they grow, you imagine all the dishes you can make with these ripe fruits. Then there is the wonderful smell of the tomatoes on the vines, a unique aroma that I have never been able to capture in a dish. Anne-Marie tends to this forest of tomatoes.

For me, it is all about the variety as it makes the difference between a dish that is OK and one that is excellent. So let me explain …

Tomato salad: of the hundreds of varieties that I have tried in salads, the best are the Black Russian, Coeur de Boeuf, Marmande, Noire de Crimée and the Green Zebra. Why are they the best? The juice creates the acidity and flavour and the flesh creates the sweetness and texture. It is Mother Nature's perfect balance of flesh and juice (with the help of an expert gardener). Oh, and never keep them in the fridge.

Stuffing: tomatoes can be stuffed with rice, quinoa, seeds, grains, mincemeat and fish and baked in a hot oven for 20–30 minutes. The tomato should have thick walls to keep in the stuffing and, for this, I like Coeur de Boeuf (few seeds and you can use some of the flesh as part of the stuffing), Marmande and Costoluto Fiorentino.

Grilling and baking: most mornings I have my breakfast at Le Manoir and often I celebrate bacon and egg and tomatoes, which are halved, drizzled with a little olive oil and baked or grilled. My favourite varieties for this are Black Russian and Cherokee Purple.

Tomato sauce: the perfect sauce requires tomatoes that have little acidity and juice and as much flesh as possible. Why? If there is little juice and a lot of flesh the tomatoes will create a purée very quickly and there will be lots of it. For sauce, the best tomatoes are Italian, such as San Marzano and the Roma (plum).

Packed with nutrients, especially when fully ripe, the tomato is also rich in lycopene, which can help to fight cancer and lowers the risk of heart disease. When the tomato is cooked, the lycopene is more easily absorbed by the body. Good food and nutrition are friends, they work together.

Fish Pie

PREP 10 MINS / COOK 1 HOUR 20 MINS

Oh, the glorious fish pie! Piping hot, creamy and with a well-browned, crispy crust of mashed potato, it's incredibly satisfying, especially in the chilly months. In my recipe, the sauce is cooked and then poured over the raw fish before baking. This ensures that the fish is perfect. The sauce can be made in advance and kept in the fridge. Or assemble the pie, minus the topping, and freeze. Find a suitably sized ovenproof dish, and you're away …

SERVES 4–6

300g pollock
300g salmon

For the potato topping
1kg Desirée or Maris
   Piper potatoes
100ml whole milk,
   warmed
100g unsalted butter,
   melted
4 pinches of sea salt flakes
6 pinches of ground
   white pepper

For the sauce
1 white onion
1 small fennel bulb
1 large leek
2 handfuls of button
   mushrooms
a handful of curly or
   flat-leaf parsley
100g unsalted butter
40g plain flour
320ml whole milk
160ml whipping cream
   (or double cream)
juice of ½ lemon
sea salt flakes and
   black pepper

Preheat the oven to 190°C/170°C fan/gas 5.

TO PREPARE Peel and quarter the potatoes and steam or boil them for 25–30 minutes, or until soft. Meanwhile, you can prepare the other ingredients for the sauce. Finely slice the onion. Dice the fennel. Halve the leek lengthways, lightly wash away any grit, and coarsely chop it. Wash the mushrooms by swirling them for 10 seconds in cold water with a dash of lemon juice, and then drain them. Chop them in halves or quarters, depending on size. Roughly chop the parsley.

When the potatoes are cooked, strain in a colander and leave for a few minutes for the steam to escape. Pass the potatoes through a moulin-légumes, food mill or potato ricer – or simply mash them with a potato masher. Return the potato to the saucepan, pour in some of the milk and mix with a spatula – your mash should be fluffy and quite firm, and not wet. Add more milk if it's too firm. Next, add the butter, season with salt and pepper and stir. Taste, and correct the seasoning if need be. Cover it and put it to one side.

Now, the sauce. In a large sauté pan, over a low–medium heat, melt the butter and soften the onion, fennel, leek and mushrooms for 4–5 minutes – the idea is simply to sweat them, so stir every now and again so that they don't brown. Stir in the flour and cook for 1 minute. Increase the heat to high, pour in the milk and stir with a whisk. Cook for 2 minutes until it's thick and smooth. Stir in the cream, chopped parsley and lemon juice. Taste and adjust the seasoning as necessary.

Cut the fish into bite-sized chunks (about 2cm) and put them into a suitably sized ovenproof dish. Pour over the sauce.

Reheat the mashed potato until warm, if necessary, transfer it to a piping bag and pipe over your mix. Or spoon the mashed potato into the centre of the dish and then spread it evenly across the top of the fish and sauce. At this point you can either reserve the fish pie in the fridge where it will keep until the next day for you to bake, or store it in the freezer until required.

Bake for 30–40 minutes until the crust is golden and tantalising. Remove from the oven and allow the pie to rest for 5 minutes before serving.

Seared Sesame Tuna and Quick-pickled Fennel

PREP 5 MINS / COOK 10 MINS / SOAKING 30 MINS

The tuna is one of the fastest swimmers in the ocean, and amongst the fastest to cook in the pan. Overcook and it will be dry. This is an almost-effortless, light and healthy lunch or starter on a summer's day. The quick-pickled fennel brings a refreshing aniseed addition, and the radishes add pepperiness.

SERVES 4

4 tuna steaks (each
  about 120g)
sea salt flakes and
  black pepper
2 tablespoons olive oil
1–2 tablespoons sesame
  seeds
½ lime

*For the pickled fennel
salad*
1 fennel bulb
10 red radishes
2 dill sprigs
3 spring onions
  (optional)
2 tablespoons extra-
  virgin olive oil

For the pickle liquor
80ml water
100ml white wine
  vinegar
30g caster sugar
1 teaspoon sea salt flakes
80g ice cubes

TO PREPARE Begin with the salad. Using a mandolin slicer or sharp knife, finely slice the fennel and radish. Transfer the slices to a bowl of iced water and leave them for 30 minutes. Pick the leaves from the dill sprigs and slice the spring onions, if using.

Meanwhile, make the pickling liquor like this … Pour the water and vinegar into a small saucepan and add the sugar and salt. Over a medium heat, bring to a simmer and then remove the pan from the heat and add the ice to cool it. Put to one side.

After 30 minutes in the water, drain the fennel and radish and transfer them to a bowl. Pour the pickling liquor over the fennel and radish and toss the vegetables so they are coated. Reserve until you're ready to cook the tuna.

When it's time to cook the tuna steaks, season each side with a pinch of salt and a turn of black pepper. Brush them with the olive oil and turn them in the sesame seeds so that they are evenly coated.

Place a large non-stick sauté pan (or frying pan) on a high heat. Let it pick up some heat, and then place the tuna steaks into the hot pan. The timing depends on the thickness of the steak and you may need to lower the heat so the sesame seeds don't burn. For thin steaks, about 1 minute on each side. For thicker steaks, sear them on each side for 2–3 minutes. Transfer the seared steaks to a chopping board and leave them for a moment while you finish the salad.

Drain the fennel and radish, reserving the liquor, and add the extra-virgin olive oil, dill leaves and spring onions, if using. Toss the salad, taste and adjust the seasoning accordingly. At this point, you can add 1–2 teaspoons of the pickling liquor back to the salad if you prefer the salad more acidic.

Squeeze a little lime juice over each tuna steak. Cut the steaks into thick slices crossways and serve with the pickled fennel salad.

Mussel and Saffron Risotto

PREP 20 MINS / COOK 40 MINS

SERVES 4

For the mussels
1kg fresh mussels
1 onion
2 bay leaves
2 thyme sprigs
1 tablespoon unsalted
  butter
100ml dry white wine

For the risotto
1 garlic clove
1 tablespoon unsalted
  butter
200g carnaroli rice
  (or arborio)
2 bay leaves
a couple of pinches
  of saffron powder
  or strands
pinch of cayenne pepper
2 pinches of sea salt flakes
100ml dry white wine
300ml water (or fish
  stock)

To finish
50g Parmigiano-
  Reggiano cheese
2 teaspoons unsalted
  butter, at room
  temperature
a handful of coarsely
  chopped flat-leaf parsley
100g cooked peas
  (optional)
a handful of baby-leaf
  spinach (optional)
½ lemon, for squeezing

Mussels and saffron are united harmoniously in this classic risotto. There's no need for that constant stirring. Instead, the rice is stirred towards the end of the cooking time to activate the starches, a trick you can use with any risotto you make.

TO PREPARE First, the mussels. Ensure that all the mussels are tightly closed and not damaged before you begin to cook; any mussels that are damaged or open should be discarded. The preparation can be done in advance. Wash the mussels in a large bowl and under cold running water. Mussels that float at this stage are not very fresh, so discard them. Remove any barnacles and beards, but don't scrub the shells as this can end up colouring the cooking juices. Drain.

Finely chop the onion and peeled garlic and grate the cheese.

In a large saucepan over a medium heat, sweat half the onion, the bay leaves and thyme in the butter for 1 minute. Increase the heat to high, add the mussels, pour in the wine, cover with a lid and cook for 3 minutes.

Drain in a sieve over a large bowl and discard any mussels that have not opened. Reserve the cooking juices, you will need about 200ml to make the risotto. Once the mussels have cooled, pick the mussels from their shells, leaving a few in their shells for decoration, and put them all aside.

Now, to the risotto … Melt the butter in a large saucepan on a medium heat. Add the remaining onion, cover with a lid and cook for 2–3 minutes, until the onion is translucent. Add the garlic and stir in the rice. Add the bay leaves, saffron and cayenne pepper and lightly season with salt. Stir and continue to cook on a medium heat for 2 minutes, until the grains of rice are shiny.

Pour in the wine and let it boil for 30 seconds – bubble, bubble – and stir. Pour in the mussel cooking liquor and the water or fish stock and stir again. Now cook on the gentlest simmer, with just a single bubble breaking the surface. Cover with a lid and leave for 20 minutes, but it mustn't boil.

Now it's time for 5 minutes of some serious and fast stirring. At full speed, stir the risotto. The grains rub against each other, extracting the starch, and this gives the rice its creaminess. Yet every grain remains whole, unbroken. Taste – the rice should have a slight bite.

Add the cheese, butter and parsley to the risotto, along with the cooked peas and spinach, if using, all the cooked mussels and a strong squeeze of lemon. Stir, taste and correct the seasoning just before serving.

Crayfish and Crab Gratin

PREP 5 MINS / COOK 30 MINS

A creamy, comforting dish that's just right as a TV dinner (or lunch). The mixture can be transferred to small dishes or four freezer bags for quick, individual meals on the go. By using a shallow dish, the filling cooks by the time the top is golden and crisp. If using a deep gratin dish, it may be best to bake it in the oven and then finish under the grill.

SERVES 4

90g strong mature
  Cheddar cheese
200g dried macaroni
30g unsalted butter
30g plain flour
300ml whole milk
100g crabmeat
70ml whipping cream
  (or double cream)
sea salt and black pepper
½ lemon
250g crayfish tails, cooked

For the topping
50g Parmigiano-
  Reggiano cheese
a handful of breadcrumbs
  or crumbled plain
  crackers (optional)

TO PREPARE Grate the cheeses.

Cook the macaroni following the instructions on the packet. Drain it in a colander and refresh it under cold running water for 1 minute. Put the pasta to one side (or cover and refrigerate until required).

Next, the sauce, which doesn't take long and can be made while the macaroni is bubbling away. In a large saucepan over a medium heat, melt the butter, add the flour and stir to form a paste (this is a roux, pronounced roo, as in kanga). Continue to cook for 2–3 minutes.

Remove the pan from the heat, pour in the milk, slowly mix with a whisk to blend the paste and return the pan to the heat. Increase the heat to high and bring to a gentle simmer, stirring continuously with a whisk to remove lumps. See how the sauce has thickened, and now let it simmer gently for 1–2 minutes, stirring as necessary. There you have your silky, smooth béchamel sauce.

Remove the pan from the heat and while the sauce is still hot, stir in the Cheddar and crabmeat, pour in the cream and season with a couple of generous pinches of salt and a few turns of pepper. Add a couple of squeezes of lemon. Add the cooked pasta and the crayfish tails and gently stir them in. Taste and adjust the seasoning accordingly. (At this stage, the gratin can be covered and refrigerated, or stored in the freezer, until required, but defrost fully before cooking.)

The final bit … Preheat the grill to high. Transfer the mixture to a suitably-sized ovenproof serving dish – as I say, I prefer to use a shallow dish. Top it with the grated Parmigiano-Reggiano and, if using, sprinkle with the breadcrumbs (or crumbled crackers).

Place the dish under the grill, reduce the heat to medium and cook for 10–12 minutes, until it is golden on top (keep an eye on it – no burning, please). Alternatively, bake in an oven preheated to 160°C/140°C fan/ gas 3 and finish under the grill, browning the gratin to your liking.

Mussels

Mussels were a rare treat when I was growing up beside the forests of Franche-Comté, many miles from the sea. Maman Blanc, I remember, served them sometimes at Christmas as a canapé. Along the coast of France, of course, they form the basis of dishes. Brittany has Moules Farcies – the shells are stuffed with herb-garlic butter and swiftly baked in a very hot oven. Visit the southwest of France, where mussels have been cultivated since the thirteenth century, and you may well be offered La Mouclade Vendéenne, a mussel stew often made with saffron, cream and Cognac.

Meanwhile, here is a trio of recipes. That classic Normandy dish of Moules Marinière, where sometimes the region's cider replaces the wine, is such an amazing dish and I'd never dare take it off the menu at Brasserie Blanc. For Moules Provençal, the mussels are generously covered with garlic and parsley butter, coated with seasoned breadcrumbs, and then baked and served in the shell – a dish in itself, though it can also be served as canapés. Then there is a Thai-inspired dish of mussels with lemongrass, lime and coconut milk.

Plenty to put you in mussel heaven.

PREPARING THE MUSSELS FOR THESE DISHES

The secret, as ever, is in the freshness of the mussels. A fresh mussel is shiny, closed and heavy with seawater. All mussels should be tightly closed before you begin to cook; any mussels that are not should be discarded. The preparation can be done in advance. Wash the mussels in a large bowl and under cold running water. Mussels that float at this stage are not very fresh, so discard them. Remove any barnacles and beards, but don't scrub the shells as this can end up colouring the cooking juices. Drain.

Moules Marinière

PREP 10 MINS / COOK LESS THAN 10 MINS

SERVES 4

1 small white onion
3 tablespoons flat-leaf
  parsley
1.8kg fresh mussels
120g unsalted butter
4 bay leaves
8 thyme sprigs
100ml dry white wine
2 tablespoons double
  cream

TO PREPARE Finely dice the onion. Coarsely chop the parsley. Prepare the mussels, as opposite.

In a large saucepan over a high heat, melt the butter. Add the onion, bay leaves and thyme, stir and then pour in the wine. Bring to the boil, add the mussels and cover with a tight-fitting lid.

Cook for 2–3 minutes until the mussels open. Stir in the cream and chopped parsley.

Serve with good French bread.

Mussels with Lemongrass, Lime and Coconut

PREP 10 MINS / COOK 10 MINS

SERVES 4

1 banana shallot or
  ½ onion
1 lemongrass stick
2cm piece of fresh
  root ginger
2 or 3 red chillies,
  to your taste
1.8kg fresh mussels
3 tablespoons olive oil
1 teaspoon Madras
  curry powder
200ml coconut milk
4 pinches of sea salt
½ bunch of roughly
  chopped coriander,
  to finish

TO PREPARE Finely slice the shallot or onion. Smash the lemongrass stick, and coarsely chop it. Grate or finely slice the peeled ginger. Halve the chillies, and remove and discard the seeds. Prepare the mussels, as opposite.

In a large saucepan, heat the olive oil on a medium heat. Add the shallot, lemongrass, ginger, chilli and curry powder, stir, cover with a lid and cook for 1–2 minutes until soft.

Increase the heat to high and, when the pan is nice and hot, add the mussels. Pour in the coconut milk, add the salt, cover with the lid again and bring to the boil. By now all the shellfish should have opened. Discard any mussels that haven't opened. Sprinkle over the coriander.

Serve with crusty bread or a bowl of fluffy jasmine rice.

Moules Provençal

PREP 10 MINS / COOK 15 MINS

SERVES 4

1 small white onion
1.8kg fresh mussels
2 tablespoons unsalted
  butter
2 bay leaves
4 thyme sprigs
100ml dry white wine

For the herb butter
2 handfuls of curly or
  flat-leaf parsley
1 garlic clove
1 shallot
60g breadcrumbs, plus
  extra to dust the
  mussels before grilling
180g unsalted butter
4 tablespoons water

TO PREPARE Coarsely chop the parsley, peeled garlic and the shallot. Finely dice the onion. Prepare the mussels, as previously. Now you are well prepared.

To make the herb butter, blend the parsley, garlic and shallot with the breadcrumbs, butter and water in a food processor, or with a stick blender, to a smooth paste. Transfer to a bowl and keep at room temperature.

Melt the butter in a large saucepan over a high heat. Add the onion, bay leaves and thyme, reduce the heat to medium, stir, cover with a lid and cook for 1 minute or until the onion has softened.

Increase the heat to high, add the mussels, pour in the white wine, cover with a lid and cook for 2–3 minutes – enough time for the mussels to open.

Drain the mussels in a colander and over a bowl, saving the cooking juices (which can be stored in the freezer and used in another dish, such as risotto). Carefully remove one half of each mussel shell and discard it – this leaves the mussel flesh inside one half of the shell, ready for the herb butter topping. Place the mussels on a baking tray and preheat the grill to high.

Spread about a teaspoon of the herb butter onto each mussel. Use the back of the spoon to smoothly spread the butter over the whole of the mussel. Top with a pinch or two of breadcrumbs. Place the tray of mussels on the middle shelf of the grill for 3–5 minutes, until the breadcrumb topping is crisp and golden. Serve hot, with crusty bread and a rosé from Provence.

Pan-fried Fillet of Salmon, Chive-butter Sauce and Wilted Spinach

PREP 5 MINS / COOK 10 MINS

SERVES 4

For the wilted spinach (optional)
1 garlic clove
2 tablespoons water
400g spinach
1 tablespoon olive oil
  or unsalted butter
2 pinches of sea salt flakes
4 turns of ground
  black pepper

For the salmon
4 salmon fillets, skin on
  and pin boned
2 tablespoons sunflower
  or vegetable oil
sea salt flakes and ground
  black pepper

For the chive-butter sauce
½ shallot
1 tablespoon chives
1 small tomato (optional)
1 teaspoon unsalted
  butter
80ml water
30–40g unsalted butter,
  cold and diced
juice of ½ lemon
pinch of sea salt flakes

VARIATIONS

Blanched parsley, spring greens or sorrel would also be a good accompaniment.

The slow-cooked sizzled skin of this salmon is crispy and tastes delicious, while the flesh of the fish is luxuriously rich. It's an easy dish, and the chive-butter sauce can be made while the salmon cooks.

TO PREPARE Finely chop the peeled garlic, shallot and chives. Deseed the tomato, if using, and dice it.

First, prepare the spinach, if using. Pour the water into a large pan and add the spinach. Add the olive oil or butter and the garlic and season with salt and pepper. Cover with a lid. Now it is ready to cook.

Pat the salmon fillets dry with kitchen paper. Pour the oil into a large non-stick frying pan on a medium heat and when the oil is hot, add the salmon fillets, skin-side down. You'll hear that reassuring sizzle. Very fresh fish will arc upwards at this point, so use a fish slice or wide spatula to press down the fillets for a few seconds so they stay flat against the pan.

Cook the fillets for 7–8 minutes, depending on their thickness, until the skin is crisp and golden. If the skin colours too quickly, reduce the heat. I want you to hear just a gentle sizzle, as the skin browns and crisps up.

Meanwhile, make the sauce while the salmon is in the pan. In a small round-bottomed saucepan on a medium heat, sweeten the shallot in the teaspoon of butter for 1 minute without colouring. Add the water, bring to the boil and whisk in the diced cold butter to create an emulsion. Remove the pan from the heat and add the lemon juice, chopped chives, diced tomato and a pinch of salt, to taste.

While the salmon is cooking, you can also cook the spinach, if using, on a medium–high heat for 1–2 minutes.

Now season the salmon fillets on the flesh side with salt and pepper, and turn them over to continue cooking for 1 minute. Then remove the pan from the heat and leave the fillets in the pan. Gently reheat the chive butter sauce if necessary.

If using spinach, place it in the middle of each plate. Lay a salmon fillet on top of the spinach and spoon around the hot chive-butter sauce. Serve.

Flash-fried Squid, Fennel and Rocket Salad

PREP 20 MINS / COOK 5 MINS / SOAK 2 HOURS / MARINATE 30 MINS

To me, there are only two ways to cook squid. Either griddled (or flash-fried) for a minute or so. Or 2 hours of slow cooking. The first barely cooks the flesh, creating a mellow texture (not elastic), and the griddle adds its own fabulous charred effect. Meanwhile, the slow cooking releases the hidden sweetness of the squid, and tenderises it. There is no in-between. Ideally, buy fresh squid from your fishmonger in the summer months. Supermarkets also sell excellent-quality frozen squid pouches, which have been prepared for cooking. Flavour aside, there are many nutritional advantages to eating more squid. Squid is high in protein, low in calories and rich in minerals and vitamins.

SERVES 4

4 small squid (if frozen, defrost in the fridge overnight)

For the fennel and rocket salad (it benefits from being prepared a day in advance)
1 large fennel bulb
4 handfuls of rocket leaves
a handful of coriander leaves

For the marinade (can be prepared a day in advance)
10g piece of fresh root ginger
½ mild red chilli or a pinch of chilli powder
2 tablespoons palm or dark muscovado sugar
juice of ¼ lime
2–3 tablespoons olive oil
pinch of sea salt flakes

For the Thai dressing (can be prepared a day in advance)
150g Thai green curry paste (shop-bought)
6 tablespoons water

TO PREPARE Slice the fennel very finely – a mandolin is ideal for this job, and a wise investment. Place the sliced fennel in a large bowl of iced water for a minimum of 2 hours to allow them to curl up. If you can do this overnight, even better. Why? The water enters the pockets of the fennel and the shock of the iced water helps the fennel to change shape. You'll have the drama of beautiful fennel sculptures. Separately, the water tempers the aniseed flavour and makes for crunchier fennel. When it is time to remove the fennel from the water, pat it dry with kitchen paper.

If using fresh squid, your fishmonger will prepare it for you. And if frozen, defrost it overnight in the fridge. Then wash it and cut the squid pouch lengthways along the middle. Wash and pat dry. Score the inside in a criss-cross pattern. This will help the heat to penetrate the squid.

Finely slice the peeled ginger and the chilli and grate the palm sugar.

Add the ginger, chilli and palm sugar to a bowl, along with a strong squeeze of the lime quarter. Add the olive oil and salt. Toss the prepared squid in the marinade and leave to marinate for a minimum of 30 minutes.

To make the dressing, in a bowl mix the Thai green paste with the water. Mix the fennel with the rocket and coriander, add a third of the Thai green dressing and toss well.

The griddle pan must be very hot indeed to ensure quick cooking and to char the squid. (If it is not hot enough, you risk boiling the squid in its own juices. If the squid is overcooked it will become tough and rubbery. This high heat cooking can be a bit smoky, so put your extractor on full and remember, there's no oil being used here.)

Place the squid on the hot griddle, scored-side down. Cook for about 30 seconds, turn, and cook for a further 30 seconds, until nicely charred.

Place the fennel and rocket salad on each plate and top with the grilled squid. Put the remaining dressing in a bowl for guests to help themselves.

My love for
FENNEL

With its aniseed scent and flavours, fennel is one of those love-it or hate-it vegetables. I happen to love it and can remember the moment when I first laid eyes on it. I was twelve years old and in a bustling marketplace in the South of France when I saw a pyramid of fennel bulbs on a stall. It was my first visit to the South of France, and I was staying with my best friend, René, as he and his family had moved from Franche-Comté to live near the Mediterranean. Back at home, René's mother made a fantastic fish soup that included fennel, some saffron threads and a dash of pastis.

Then, and ever since, fennel has featured in a few 'first' moments of my life. For instance, when I was a waiter at the Rose Revived in the early 1970s, David the chef invited me to make a few dishes when service was quiet. I grilled baby turbot on a bed of fennel, orange, lemon and rosemary, with lots of olive oil. That was the first time I cooked for paying customers. Later, when I had my first restaurant, Les Quat'Saisons, Jenny and I took the children to Provence, our first family holiday, and I raided the hedgerows, packing the car with wild fennel to bring home.

Every part of the vegetable can be eaten, including the roots, which should be braised for two to three hours so they become tender and delicious. The feathery ferns are a tasty garnish, or a sorbet. The large bulb is fabulous in salads, pan-fried, roasted, grilled, pickled.

Pan-fried Slip Sole

PREP 5 MINS / COOK 15 MINS

Natalia, as well as having a master's degree in nutrition, has also perfected the skill of cooking simple food. When I first went to her home, this was not the case. I was horrified when I opened the fridge. There were a couple of organic tomatoes. My heart was lifted by the sight of a few bottles of Krug, neatly stacked. There was no salt and pepper, no bread, butter and cheese (though I found the best extra-virgin olive oil). Things have changed. Today, Natalia is not only the nutritionist at the Raymond Blanc Cookery School, she also does the best Dover sole, or rather slip sole, which is a small Dover sole, and an occasional treat that I'd recommend. Often when I return home late, I enter the house, tired and stressed, and then I smell the deep-rich scents of a beurre noisette. Natalia is cooking the slip sole. It can be served with wilted spinach, new potatoes or any vegetable you wish, including broad beans, another of Natalia's specialities (see page 50). This recipe shows that by simply pan-frying fish (or meat or vegetables) in a small amount of butter, a sumptuous flavour is achieved, and all that is needed is a little water and lemon to make the jus. For budget-friendly alternatives, there are fantastic substitutes, such as plaice, lemon sole, cod or haddock.

SERVES 2

2 slip sole
30g unsalted butter
100ml water
juice of ½ lemon
a few pinches of
  sea salt flakes
a few turns of ground
  black pepper
1 tablespoon finely
  chopped curly or
  flat-leaf parsley, to
  finish (optional)

TO PREPARE Pat dry the fish with kitchen paper.

Over a medium heat, melt the butter in a large sauté or frying pan (about 25cm diameter) – just let it foam and when it stops foaming and is beautifully golden, lay the sole in the pan so that they are in the opposite direction to one another. Listen to the sound of the pan – it should be singing a gentle simmer and then you know you will have the most heavenly pan juices. If the heat is too low, the juices will escape from the fish; if it's too high, you'll burn the fish and butter. So adjust the heat as necessary, or remove the pan from the heat for a few seconds.

Pan-fry the fish for 4–5 minutes until golden – resist any urge to move the fish at this stage. Turn and fry for a further 4–5 minutes. Keep listening to the sizzling, adjusting the heat as necessary.

Pour in the water and let it bubble away and emulsify with the butter. Squeeze the lemon over each sole, season, sprinkle with the chopped parsley, if using, and spoon over the glorious sauce made from the cooking juices, lemon and butter. Serve.

'Please let a joint of meat rest
for at least 20 minutes per
kilogramme. Resting creates
tenderness and succulence
and releases more juices for
your jus, sauce or gravy.'

MEAT DISHES

Spicy Chicken Paillard

155

Marmalade Duck

156

Pan-fried Pork Chops and Steamed
Kale with Apple Sauce

159

Tartiflette

160

Onion and Bacon Tart

163

Roast Chicken with Pommes Purée

166

Chicken Braised with
White Wine and Mustard

169

Pappardelle with Mushrooms,
Bacon and Crème Fraîche

170

Slow-cooked Pork Belly with
Steamed Pointed Cabbage and
Cumin and Pan-fried Parsnips
173

Steak Maman Blanc and Steak,
Red Wine Jus with Sauté
Potatoes and Bacon
177

Roast Butternut Squash, Chorizo,
Chickpeas, Tahini Dressing
181

Beef Braised in Red Wine
182

Pithivier
185

Pan-fried Chicken Breast,
Morel Sauce
186

Spicy Chicken Paillard

PREP 15 MINS / COOK 10 MINS / MARINATE 30 MINS

There is a certain simplicity to this dish and often I cook it at home. The fillets of chicken breast are butterflied, which is fun. And then they are bashed. Which is even more fun. That's the 'paillard' part. The spicy marinade deserves credit for the rest of the work and you'll have the tenderest, most succulent chicken, which is perfect with a salad, such as the Courgette Salad on page 94. It's so tasty, and I am making myself hungry as I write about it! If the weather is kind, then this is a must-try dish for the barbecue. Otherwise, it's one for your cooker indoors.

SERVES 4

4 boneless chicken breast fillets, skinless

2 teaspoons ground cumin

2 teaspoons ground turmeric

2 teaspoons curry powder

2 pinches of chilli powder

juice of 1 lemon

3 tablespoons extra-virgin olive oil

2 pinches of sea salt flakes

2 turns of ground black pepper

TO PREPARE To butterfly the chicken breast fillets, on a clean surface or board, lay a chicken breast fillet with the thickest part of the fillet closest to you, and the pointed part away from you. Using a sharp knife, slice through the fillet, but not quite all the way, so that it opens up like a book and is heart or butterfly shaped. Place the fillet to one side and repeat the process with the three remaining fillets.

Now make the marinade. Place all the remaining ingredients in a bowl, mix with a fork and put to one side.

Put a butterflied fillet in the middle of the board and cover it with a sheet of non-pvc clingfilm. Use a rolling pin to bash the chicken, bashing with just enough force to flatten the chicken breast to about 1cm. Put the flattened fillet to one side and repeat the bashing with the remaining fillets until they are all flattened.

Transfer the chicken to a large dish and pour the marinade over the fillets, ensuring they are thoroughly coated. Cover the dish with clingfilm and refrigerate, leaving the chicken to marinate for at least 30 minutes (or preferably overnight).

Cook the marinated chicken fillets for 4–5 minutes on each side in any of these ways: on a large griddle pan; pan-fried in a large non-stick pan; grilled under a medium–high grill; or cooked on the barbecue, if the weather permits you.

VARIATIONS

• The marinade can be used for other cuts of chicken, such as thigh, or other meats. Or use it to marinate any root or firm-fleshed vegetables, such as courgettes, turnips, carrots or chicory.

• Rather than marinating the chicken, brush it with olive oil, salt and pepper and a little lemon juice. Or make a soy-based marinade or one with yoghurt and curry spices.

• If you don't want to butterfly the chicken, skinless chicken breast fillets can be marinated whole: score them, cover with the marinade and refrigerate until it's time to cook.

Marmalade Duck

PREP 5 MINS / COOK 30 MINS

Duck loves to be paired with sweet fruit, as you will see with this hearty treat. The skin-side of the breast fillets are slowly rendered in the pan – a cooking technique in which the fat almost melts away, leaving crisp, paper-thin skin. True, rendering can be done rapidly, on a high heat in half the time, but it's all sizzle, sizzle, spit, spit, spit. I far prefer this soft, gentle approach. Marmalade Duck goes well with any of the following: Quick Carrots Vichy (see page 237), Steamed Pointed Cabbage and Cumin (see page 174) or Roasted Sweet Potatoes with Lentils (see page 198).

SERVES 4

4 boneless duck breast
  fillets (each approx.
  160g), skin on
sea salt flakes and black
  pepper
4 tablespoons orange
  marmalade
1 tablespoon water
dash of red wine vinegar

VARIATION

I am still thinking
of duck with sweet
fruits … Instead of
marmalade sauce,
try a blueberry sauce.
Crush 2 handfuls
of blueberries in a
saucepan and pour
in 40ml red wine and
40ml ruby port. On
a medium–high heat,
reduce the liquid to
a syrup. Serve the
sauce with the duck
breast fillets.

TO PREPARE Score the duck breasts by running a razor-sharp knife in diagonal lines across the skin and into the fat of each fillet, leaving about ½cm between the lines. Scoring takes only a moment, but it means the fat will be easily rendered, or released, during cooking. Score a diamond pattern, if you are feeling creative. *Voilà!*

Now it's time to cook, in a dry pan (with no fats). Lay the duck fillets skin-side down in a large sauté or frying pan, place the pan on the lowest heat and cook for 10–12 minutes. After about a minute, lift the fillets with a spatula, just to ensure the fillets don't stick to the pan. Here, the object is not to cook the duck. Instead, think of it as gently rendering the fat.

Now, turn up the heat to medium–high and colour the skin for 3–4 minutes. Meanwhile, season the flesh-side of each fillet with a pinch of sea salt flakes and a turn of black pepper.

Turn the fillets so they are now skin-side up and, again, reduce the heat to low. Cook like this for a further 8–10 minutes. Gentle, gentle, barely a sound from the pan.

Next, increase the heat to medium and cook for a further 1–2 minutes to colour the duck meat. Remove the pan from the heat and leave the duck breast fillets to rest in the pan while you make the marmalade sauce. The duck will stay warm and does not need to be covered with foil.

In a small saucepan, warm the marmalade. Add the water and dash of vinegar. If the sauce is too thick, add a little more water. Taste and season with the salt and pepper accordingly.

Spoon the hot sauce onto a warm serving platter. There are now two ways of serving the duck breast fillets: either whole or carve the fillets and lay the slices on top of the sweet-tangy sauce. Retain the duck fat from the pan and store it in the fridge – it's the best and tastiest fat for sautéing and for roasting potatoes.

Pan-fried Pork Chops and Steamed Kale with Apple Sauce

PREP 5 MINS / COOK 25 MINS

This is a multitask dish. The five-minute apple sauce is fresh-tasting and nutritious. Meanwhile, the pork chops are placed into the hot pan when the butter is foaming and just about to turn brown. That way, the chops will cook – slowly, slowly – to a dark amber colour, and the juices will stick to the pan. These, with the addition of water, will give you the most marvellous jus.

SERVES 2

2 large double-bone
   pork chops
3 pinches of sea salt flakes
4 turns of ground
   black pepper
1 tablespoon unsalted
   butter
2 thyme sprigs
100ml water

For the apple sauce
2 Braeburn apples
   (or Bramley for a faster
   apple sauce. It has
   higher acidity and water
   content and will be
   done in 5 minutes)
2 tablespoons water

For the steamed kale
4 large handfuls of kale
100ml water
generous pinch of sea
   salt flakes
1 tablespoon unsalted
   butter

TO PREPARE First, the apple sauce. Peel and core the apples, and chop them into pieces of about 2cm.

In a medium saucepan with a lid and on a medium heat, cook the apple pieces in the water for 6–8 minutes, stirring occasionally, until the apple pieces are soft enough to be broken with the back of a fork. Remove the pan from the heat and leave the sauce to cool until ready to serve. It can be blended to a purée or left as it is, with more texture than a purée.

While the apple sauce is cooking, put the kale in a medium-sized saucepan, add the water, season with the salt and place the butter on top of the kale. Cover the pan with a lid, and leave it for now.

Next, season the pork chops with the salt and pepper. In a large frying pan, and over a medium heat, melt the butter and when it is foaming (at the beurre noisette stage) add the thyme sprigs and place the pork chops in the pan. Cook the chops for 7 minutes on each side, until beautifully golden and appetising.

After you have turned the chops, start to cook the kale. Put the kale pan, covered with a lid, on a high heat. Very quickly the kale begins to steam and it will take 3–4 minutes to cook. Drain the kale, and taste for seasoning.

In the final minute of the chops frying, pour the water into the hot pan. Sizzle, sizzle, sizzle – don't you simply love the reassuring sound of near-completion!

Divide the steamed kale between the two plates, place a chop on top, and spoon the hot pan juices over the chop. Serve with the apple sauce.

VARIATION

Try rainbow chard or spinach instead of kale, depending on how the mood takes you.

Tartiflette

PREP 10 MINS / COOK 25 MINS

If I close my eyes, I am back there. It is way past midnight, the snow is falling heavily, and indoors a log fire crackles. My father and the other men are at a table in the dining room, playing their tarot card game, laughing and drinking my grandfather's pear or plum eau-de-vie. My mother is in the kitchen, chattering with the wives. Then she lifts her nose – she has detected that something is cooked to the point of delicious, and it is ready to come out of the oven. '*Ah, la tartiflette,*' says Maman. She opens the oven door and produces a piping-hot dish of sliced potatoes, bacon and onion in a creamy, Comté-cheesy sauce. Tartiflette is a peasant dish and the best comfort food. This is my version, finished under the grill. Of course, you can make it without cream, but I think cream is a must on this particular occasion. Enjoy tartiflette with a good white wine, preferably from the Jura region. And if you like late-night tarot, tartiflette will keep you going until breakfast.

SERVES 4

600g King Edward or
  Maris Piper potatoes
150g smoked streaky
  bacon, cold (so it's
  easy to cut)
1 large white onion
100g Comté cheese
  (preferably 12 months
  old)
1 tablespoon sunflower oil
2 thyme sprigs
pinch of sea salt
200–300ml double cream
½ handful of finely
  chopped chives,
  to garnish

TO PREPARE Peel and quarter the potatoes. Slice the cold bacon into pieces of about ½cm and dice the onion to about 1cm. Grate the Comté cheese.

Cook the potatoes in gently boiling, salted water for 15–20 minutes, or until just tender. Slice them lengthways. While the potatoes are cooking, turn to the bacon and onion …

Bring a large pan of water to the boil, add the bacon and blanch for 30 seconds. Drain and place on kitchen paper.

Heat the oil in a large sauté pan on a medium heat, add the bacon and sear it for 2–3 minutes until it is slightly crispy. Now reduce the heat to low–medium, add the onion, thyme and salt, stir, and cover with a lid. Cook for a further 4–5 minutes, stirring once or twice to prevent the onion colouring and sticking to the base of the pan.

Add the potato to the bacon and onion in the pan. Add half of the grated cheese and mix – but gently, so as not to break the potatoes too much.

Preheat the grill to medium.

Transfer the mixture from the pan to an ovenproof dish and pour in half the cream. Top with the remaining grated Comté cheese. Pour the remaining cream over the tartiflette – don't worry, the diet begins tomorrow!

Place the dish under the grill for 5 minutes until the tartiflette is golden and bubbling (please keep an eye on it – it would be a shame for it to burn, and for you to fall at this almost-final hurdle).

Sprinkle the chives over the tartiflette and serve immediately.

Onion and Bacon Tart

PREP 10 MINS / COOK 45 MINS / COOL 5–10 MINS

Onion and bacon tart is so very, very French. A bistro favourite, which also, over the centuries, has been lovingly made in the homes of my region – dairy-rich Franche-Comté. One day you must make it in yours. The good people of Lyon claim this tart to be their own (as it probably is), but it has made its way right across the east of France. Traditionally, the tart is served with a crunchy green salad, and maybe a mustard dressing. A little cheese can always be stirred into the hot mixture in the pan before baking – some grated Comté, perhaps, or crumbly pieces of Saint Agur, the blue cheese from Auvergne. As an accompanying wine, I suggest something from Burgundy, a crisp Chablis or a light Pinot Noir.

SERVES 6

1 shortcrust pastry case, precooked, about 20cm diameter (shop-bought or see page 296)

For the filling
2 large onions
150g smoked streaky bacon
50g unsalted butter
4 pinches of sea salt flakes
2 turns of ground black pepper
2 pinches of ground nutmeg
10g plain flour
100ml whole milk, cold
100g crème fraîche
3 medium eggs (preferably organic or free-range)

Preheat the oven to 180°C/160°C fan/gas 4.

TO PREPARE Halve the onions and finely slice them. Finely slice the bacon into very small lardons.

In a large sauté pan and on a medium heat, melt the butter, add the sliced onion and cover with a lid. Sauté the onion in the butter for a total of 10–12 minutes, until soft and lightly golden, but not browned. Season with the salt, pepper and nutmeg.

Meanwhile, place the lardons in a dry frying pan (no oil or fat) on a low–medium heat, and gently sauté them for 3–4 minutes, or until they are slightly browned.

Back to the onions … When they are soft and lightly golden, add the flour, stir, and continue to sauté for 1 minute. Remove the pan from the heat, pour in the cold milk, add the crème fraîche, and stir. Return the pan to the heat, bring it back to a gentle simmer, stir, and cook for 3–4 minutes.

Remove the pan from the heat and leave it to cool for 5–10 minutes. Beat the eggs and stir them into the mixture in the pan. Add half the bacon lardons, and stir again.

Pour the mixture into the precooked pastry case. Top with the remaining bacon lardons and bake in the oven for 20–25 minutes, until the tart is perfectly browned on top.

Before serving, allow the tart to cool slightly – that is when it's the best.

Roast Chicken with Pommes Purée

This recipe for a great classic bring backs childhood memories. I'd go with my father to hunt the chicken, which would be perched on the branch of a tree – proper free range. I am not suggesting you go climbing trees but, if the budget permits, roast a good-quality, free-range bird. Roast chicken is excellent with Pommes Purée (see opposite) and Quick Carrots Vichy (see page 237).

Roast Chicken

PREP 5 MINS / COOK 1 HOUR 10 MINS / REST 25 MINS (that's 15 minutes in the residual heat of the oven, plus about 10 minutes on a board, loosely covered in tinfoil, while you make the jus)

SERVES 4

8 chicken wings (2 of these can come from your chicken, if you wish)
1 small bulb of garlic
2 tablespoons groundnut or sunflower oil
1 chicken (about 1.8kg) (preferably organic or free-range)
2 tablespoons unsalted butter, softened
6 thyme sprigs
sea salt flakes and black pepper
200ml water

To thicken the jus (optional)
½ teaspoon cornflour (or arrowroot)
2 tablespoons cold water

VARIATION

A mixture of sliced truffle and butter, or sliced tarragon and butter, may be spread between the skin and breast of the chicken.

Preheat the oven to 220°C/200°C fan/gas 7.

TO PREPARE Chop each chicken wing into two pieces, cutting it at the joint. Cut the bulb of garlic in half horizontally.

Heat the oil in a roasting tin over a medium–high heat on the hob and let it pick up some heat. Add the chicken wings and sear them for 4–5 minutes, until golden. Remove the tin from the heat.

Place the chicken in the roasting tin on top of the chicken wings and halved garlic bulb. Brush the softened butter over the chicken and stuff the thyme sprigs inside the cavity. Season the bird with salt and black pepper.

Roast for a total of 1 hour–1 hour 5 minutes. After the first 30 minutes, reduce the temperature to 160°C/140°C fan/gas 3. Baste the chicken occasionally while it's roasting. After 45 minutes, pour the water into the tin.

After 1 hour–1 hour 5 minutes, remove the chicken from the oven, prop the chicken on its breast, and return it to the oven. Now turn off the oven, but leave the chicken to rest for 15 minutes in the residual heat of the oven, and with the door slightly ajar. All the juices will flow from the chicken, helping to create a delicious jus in the roasting tin.

Once the chicken has rested, check its juices run clear by inserting a skewer into the thigh (if using a thermometer, it's 75°C/170°F). Place the chicken on a carving board, loosely covered with tinfoil. Use a spoon to remove excess fat from the roasting tin. Taste the jus and correct the seasoning. You can serve it as it is, but if you wish to have a thicker sauce, do so like this ... Strain the juices and, in a saucepan, bring to a simmer. Skim away any excess fat, if necessary. Make a paste by mixing together the cornflour and cold water; second, add a spoonful of the hot jus to the paste; third, whisk the paste into the simmering jus in the saucepan.

Carve the chicken, passing the wishbone to the youngest at the table; the oldest have already seen their wishes come true. Serve with the jus.

Pommes Purée

PREP 5 MINS / COOK 30 MINS

For this dish, I like to use waxy, often yellow-fleshed varieties, such as Désirée, Belle de Fontenay or Estima.

SERVES 4

500–600g Désirée, Belle de Fontenay, Estima or Maris Piper potatoes

To finish the purée
100ml whole milk, warmed
35g unsalted butter, melted
2 generous pinches of sea salt flakes
2 pinches of ground white pepper

TO PREPARE Peel and chop the potatoes into quarters or large wedges.

Put the potatoes in a large saucepan, cover with water, bring to a boil and then reduce the heat to a gentle simmer, with the bubbles just breaking the surface. Cook like this for about 25 minutes. Test for softness.

Strain the potatoes in a colander, letting the excess steam escape for 2–3 minutes. Pass the potatoes through a moulin-légumes, food mill or a potato ricer or mash them with a potato masher. Return the purée to the same saucepan. Add the warm milk, little by little, mixing with a wooden spoon or spatula.

Stir in the melted butter, and season with the salt and pepper. Taste and correct the seasoning if necessary.

If the purée is too firm, thin with a little more milk. You know you have the perfect purée when it's fluffy, forms firm peaks and melts in your mouth. If necessary, keep warm over a pan of simmering water until you are ready to serve.

Chicken Braised with White Wine and Mustard

PREP 10 MINS / COOK 1 HOUR

I have previously referred to lapin à la moutarde in the Introduction. It's the dish of braised rabbit that brought a tear to my mother's eye, and also made her smile. She'd cry because she loved the rabbit that went to make the meal she was eating. She'd smile because lapin à la moutarde – rabbit braised with mustard, white wine and tarragon – is magical. This technique of braising or one-pot cooking can be adapted to suit any meat, and has a wonderful sauce that is herby and gently acidic. As rabbits are kept as pets, I thought it best, instead, to share my recipe for chicken braised with white wine and Dijon mustard. Any of your favourite herbs and vegetables can be added to the dish. In this one, olives and wild mushrooms are a lovely addition. I use the legs because they are the best cut for braising (the breast will become dry during cooking). To accompany this, you may like Pommes Purée (see page 167) and Wilted Spinach (see page 143).

SERVES 4–6

4 chicken thighs and
  4 drumsticks
sea salt and black pepper
½ white onion
6 garlic cloves
3 big, fat ripe tomatoes
150ml white wine
3 tablespoons sunflower
  or rapeseed oil
2 tablespoons white
  wine vinegar
4 pinches of sea salt flakes
6 whole black
  peppercorns
1 heaped tablespoon
  Dijon mustard
1 large tarragon sprig
5–6 sage leaves
100ml water

To finish
a small handful of chopped
  curly or flat-leaf parsley
  or chives

Preheat the oven to 150°C/130°C fan/gas 2.

TO PREPARE Season the chicken flesh (not the skin). Chop the onion. Finely slice the peeled garlic. Coarsely chop the tomatoes.

In a small saucepan, bring the white wine to the boil and let it boil for 10 seconds before removing from the heat. This will remove some of the alcohol but keep the freshness of the wine. Reserve.

In a large heavy-based casserole dish over a medium heat, heat the oil and then sear and lightly colour the chicken pieces for 7–8 minutes. Transfer them to a plate.

Add the onion and garlic to the casserole and sweeten them over the heat for 4–5 minutes but do not brown them. Spoon out some of the fat, pour in the vinegar – it will give off a slightly aggressive smell (you might cough), but when that aroma has faded, that's just right, and reduce it to a syrup.

Add the salt and peppercorns and the boiled white wine. Whisk in the mustard, add the chopped tomatoes, whole tarragon sprig and sage leaves. Pour in the water and return the chicken to the pan. Bring to the boil, cover with a lid (or tinfoil) and transfer to the oven to cook for 35–40 minutes, stirring occasionally. Test the chicken is cooked by taking out a leg and cutting down to the bone to check it's not pink in the centre. Taste and adjust the seasoning.

Garnish with the chopped parsley or chives and serve at the table from the pot.

Pappardelle with Mushrooms, Bacon and Crème Fraîche

PREP 5 MINS / COOK 10 MINS

You fancy an easy-to-make comfort dish. Or you are asking yourself: 'What can I cook as a midweek meal with just a few ingredients?' Either way, may I suggest this popular pasta dish, which will take you from chopping board to table in about 15 minutes. I like wide ribbons of pappardelle (the word stems from *pappare*, Italian for 'gobble' or 'scoff'), but of course it can be replaced by your favourite pasta, fresh or dried, and for a vegetarian version, omit the bacon. There are also vegan substitutes for crème fraîche.

SERVES 4

200g bacon
250g chestnut
  mushrooms
2 garlic cloves
1 thyme sprig
500g pappardelle pasta,
  fresh or dried
200g crème fraîche
sea salt flakes and
  black pepper

To finish
a handful of coarsely
  chopped flat-leaf parsley
Parmigiano-Reggiano
  cheese

TO PREPARE Chop the bacon into lardons. Finely slice the mushrooms. Finely slice the peeled garlic. Pick the leaves from the thyme. Put all of these to one side.

Place a large sauté pan on a high heat and give it a moment. Scatter the lardons into the hot pan and fry them for 3–4 minutes, until they are browned to your liking.

Add the sliced mushrooms, garlic and thyme leaves, stir and reduce to a medium heat. Place a lid on the pan and cook for 1–2 minutes – just enough time for the mushrooms to release their juices. Remove the pan from the heat, and put to one side.

Meanwhile, bring a large saucepan of water to the boil (for pasta, I salt the water with 10g of salt for every litre of water). Add the pappardelle to the boiling water and cook for 2–3 minutes if fresh or according to the packet instructions if dried. Taste to check when it's done – the pasta should have a slight bite to it.

When the pasta is in its final minute of cooking, place the frying pan with the bacon and mushrooms over a high heat. Pour in the crème fraîche, stir, bring to the boil, then reduce the heat and let the sauce simmer and thicken for a moment. Taste and, if necessary, add salt or pepper (or both) and stir.

Drain the pappardelle and add it to the creamy sauce in the pan. Remove the pan from the heat. Add the parsley and toss the pasta so that it's well coated. Taste once more, just to be sure. Serve from the pan with a sprinkling of grated Parmigiano-Reggiano.

Slow-cooked Pork Belly with Steamed Pointed Cabbage and Cumin and Pan-fried Parsnips

Pork belly is, for me, one of the great cuts of meat, and lends itself beautifully to being slow cooked. Fortunately, in Britain we have the world's finest rare pork breeds, such as Tamworth, Saddleback, Middle White and Berkshire. This is an extremely simple dish, to which you may wish to add your favourite spices. I have included recipes for my suggested accompaniments: steamed pointed cabbage with cumin, and parsnips, fried in the pan and then finished in the oven.

Slow-cooked Pork Belly

PREP 5 MINS / COOK 2½ HOURS

SERVES 4

1kg oven-ready pork belly, ribs removed
1 garlic clove
a nice, thick slice of fresh root ginger
6–8 black peppercorns
1 tablespoon muscovado sugar
300ml cold water (or chicken stock)

Preheat the oven to 150°C/130°C fan/gas 2.

TO PREPARE Remove the skin from the pork to leave a top of fat. (The skin can be sliced into four pieces, placed on a baking tray and cooked at the same time as the pork, so it becomes crackling.) Score the fat.

Finely slice the peeled garlic and grate the peeled ginger.

Mix the garlic, ginger and peppercorns with the muscovado sugar, and spread this mixture over the flesh side of the pork belly.

Place the pork belly, skin-side up, in a large casserole dish with a lid. Pour in the cold water or chicken stock, cover with a lid and transfer to the oven. Cook for 2½ hours, or until perfectly tender. (After about 2 hours, you can start to prepare the cabbage and parsnips – see page 174.) To check that the pork is just right, push the blunt handle of a tablespoon through the belly; the meat should yield easily. Strain and reserve the juices. Keep the oven on – you'll need it for the parsnips, preheated to 180°C/160°C fan/gas 4.

Return the pork belly to the casserole dish and place it under a medium grill for a few minutes, to caramelise the fat so that it is browned to your liking. Cover loosely with tinfoil while you cook the cabbage and parsnips.

Serve the slow-cooked pork belly from the casserole dish at the table, with the cabbage in a warmed large bowl or straight from the sauté pan, and the parsnips in a pan or bowl. Pour over the juices from the dish and add the pork crackling.

Steamed Pointed Cabbage and Cumin

PREP 5 MINS / COOK 5–7 MINS

Pointed cabbage is a beautiful vegetable, cooks in a few minutes and can accompany so many dishes. If you have not cooked with it, I urge you to do so. It's a must. Instead of pointed cabbage, you could also try varieties such as Chinese Leaf or Hispi.

1 pointed cabbage
20g butter
1 teaspoon cumin seeds
200ml water

TO PREPARE Chop the cabbage into quarters lengthways. Then slice each quarter into three pieces lengthways.

Place the cabbage in a sauté pan, add the butter and cumin seeds and pour in the water. Cover with a lid and cook over a medium heat for 5–7 minutes, until tender. Drain off any excess liquor.

Pan-fried Parsnips

PREP 5 MINS / COOK 15 MINS

5 parsnips
2 tablespoons unsalted
  butter
sea salt flakes and
  black pepper

TO PREPARE Peel and trim the parsnips, and slice each one into quarters lengthways.

Melt the butter over a medium heat in a large sauté pan (or frying pan), and lay the parsnips into the foaming butter. Lightly colour the parsnips all over, for about 5 minutes. Season with salt and pepper and transfer to the oven (preheated to 180°C/160°C fan/gas 4) to finish cooking for 5–8 minutes.

Steak Maman Blanc and Steak, Red Wine Jus with Sauté Potatoes and Bacon

Here are two recipes for pan-fried steak, which was a monthly treat in my childhood home. Steak Maman Blanc is named after my mother because she cooked the steak just like this, extracting the flavours of the meat and the herbs, and then adding a little water at the end in order to create the most delectable, perfumed jus. It's phenomenal! Then there is Steak with a Red Wine Jus, which is also quick and, perhaps, for a more special moment. Here you will also find my recipe for the ideal accompaniment: sauté potatoes and bacon.

Steak Maman Blanc

PREP 5 MINS / COOK 6–10 MINS

SERVES 4

4 x 225g sirloin or rump
   steaks, cut 2cm thick,
   fat trimmed
4 small pinches of sea
   salt flakes
coarsely ground black
   pepper
40g unsalted butter
200ml water

Remove the steaks from the fridge at least 30 minutes before cooking. Season each side of the steaks with the salt and grind the black pepper over them – be generous with it. Firmly press the salt and pepper into the steaks.

On a medium heat, in a large frying pan, put the butter and let it melt and foam. Then, when the butter starts to turn light gold and nutty, you know that the heat is just right to sear and slowly brown the meat. So now is the time to lay the steaks into the butter and increase the heat to medium–high in order to keep things nice and hot.

FOR RARE: cook 1 minute on each side.

FOR MEDIUM-RARE: cook for 2 minutes on each side.

FOR MEDIUM: cook for 3 minutes on each side, turning twice.

When you turn the steaks, keep each of them in the same spot in the pan.

To test if the steak is cooked to your liking, press the meat with your forefinger. For rare, it should be soft and your finger will not leave an imprint; medium will feel quite firm, because the fibres will be cooked.

Now, using tongs, transfer the steaks to a warm plate. Put the pan back on a medium–high heat and pour the water into the hot pan – sizzle, bubble, boil. The butter and water will create an emulsion. Scrape the base of the pan with a spatula or wooden spoon to release the caramelised residue, adding flavour and colour to this succulent juice. Pour the juice onto the steaks and serve immediately with the sauté potatoes.

Steak, Red Wine Jus

PREP 5 MINS / COOK 8–12 MINS

SERVES 4

1 shallot
200g field mushrooms
a small handful of curly
    or flat-leaf parsley,
    stalks on (optional)
300ml inexpensive red
    wine (such as Côtes
    du Rhône)
4 x 225g sirloin or rump
    steaks, cut 2cm thick,
    fat trimmed
60g unsalted butter, cold
sea salt flakes and
    coarsely ground
    black pepper

For a more stylish steak experience, you may like to serve it with a red wine jus. It's extremely easy. Simply follow the same method as for Steak Maman Blanc (see previously), and then make the jus at the end.

TO PREPARE Finely chop the shallot. Wash the mushrooms by swirling them for 10 seconds in a bowl of cold water. Drain them, pat dry with kitchen paper and dice. Finely chop the parsley by rolling it and chopping with its stalks. Open the bottle of wine and, yes, taste.

Follow the same preparation and cooking method as for Steak Maman Blanc, seasoning and cooking in 40g of the butter. However, when you remove the steaks from the pan, place the pan back on a medium–high heat and add the shallot and mushroom. Cook for 1 minute and then pour in the red wine and reduce by half. Whisk in the remaining 20g of cold butter. Taste and correct the seasoning.

Spoon the mushrooms over each steak, pour the red wine jus on top and sprinkle over the parsley, if using. Serve with the sauté potatoes.

Sauté Potatoes and Bacon

PREP 5 MINS / COOK 20 MINS

SERVES 4

400g potatoes

For the persillade
30g flat-leaf parsley
a small handful of chervil
4 tarragon leaves
1 banana shallot or
    ½ white onion
1 garlic clove

To finish
100g smoked bacon
    (or bacon lardons)
2 tablespoons rapeseed oil
20g unsalted butter
pinch of sea salt
2 turns of ground black
    pepper

Perfect with any pan-fried or grilled steak.

TO PREPARE Peel and dice the potatoes into about 2cm cubes. Chop the bacon into lardons. Chop the parsley, chervil and the tarragon leaves. Finely chop the shallot (or onion) and finely slice the peeled garlic.

First, make the persillade. Mix all the ingredients together in a bowl. Reserve.

In a large saucepan and on a high heat, simmer the potatoes in boiling water for 5 minutes, drain in a colander and put to one side.

Heat the oil in a large frying pan on a high heat, add the bacon lardons and lightly caramelise them. Add the blanched potatoes, and then add the butter. Season with salt and black pepper and cook for 10 minutes, stirring about once every minute, until golden brown all over.

Spoon out any excess fat and stir in the persillade. Taste and adjust the seasoning if necessary. Serve with the steak.

Roast Butternut Squash, Chorizo, Chickpeas, Tahini Dressing

PREP 15 MINS / COOK 20 MINS

The word squash is said to derive from the Native American *askutasquash*, meaning 'eaten raw'. It is indeed a fruit, technically, though few of us eat it raw. A cousin of the pumpkin, squash is so versatile and goes well with meat, game and fish, and can be steamed, stuffed, grilled, griddled … For this recipe, the squash is quartered and then roasted, creating an intensity of flavours: earthy, sweet and nutty. For a vegetarian meal in itself, simply omit the chorizo.

SERVES 4

100g chorizo
1 butternut squash
2 tablespoons olive oil
4 pinches of sea salt flakes
8 turns of ground
  black pepper
2 thyme sprigs
1 tin (400g) chickpeas

For the tahini dressing
a few coriander sprigs
a few curly or flat-leaf
  parsley sprigs
60g tahini
80g Greek yoghurt
1 teaspoon honey
¼ lemon
pinch of paprika
pinch of sea salt flakes
4 turns of ground
  black pepper

For the garnish (optional)
1 tablespoon pumpkin
  seeds, toasted
1 teaspoon sesame seeds,
  toasted

Preheat the oven to 180°C/160°C fan/gas 4.

TO PREPARE Dice the chorizo and put it to one side. Chop the squash into quarters, and cut away the hard skin. Finely chop the coriander and parsley sprigs.

Place the squash pieces in a roasting tin and toss them with the olive oil, salt and pepper. Roast for 10 minutes. Add the chorizo and thyme to the tin and continue to roast for a further 10 minutes.

Remove the tin from the oven, add the chickpeas and toss them in the chorizo roasting juices so they are coated. Now leave to cool while you make the tahini dressing.

In a medium bowl, whisk together the tahini, yoghurt and honey. Add the coriander and parsley to the bowl with the juice of the lemon quarter, along with the paprika, salt and pepper. Taste and adjust the seasoning, if necessary. Reserve.

On a large plate, place the roasted squash pieces and scatter the chorizo and chickpeas around. Spoon the tahini dressing onto the plate and, if using toasted seeds, scatter these over the plate. Finish with any chorizo-flavoured oil from the roasting tray and serve with crusty bread.

Beef Braised in Red Wine

PREP 15 MINS / COOK 3½ HOURS

A classic of French home cooking for special occasions, if you make this one dish, you'll be making many others using the same techniques. This casserole can be cooked a day in advance, and then reheated. The low oven temperature is crucial, helping to break down the fibres of the beef so that the meat becomes meltingly tender within this slow exchange of flavours. Yes, a whole bottle of wine is required, but not an expensive one and, as you will taste, the wine is essential. To simplify the process, I have not marinated the beef. However, for richer flavours – and an authentic boeuf bourguignon – the raw beef and vegetables can be left to marinate in the reduced wine overnight in the fridge. A gorgeous purée of potatoes (see page 167) is the perfect side dish.

SERVES 6

750ml full-bodied red wine (such as Shiraz or Cabernet Sauvignon)
1 large onion (or a dozen baby onions, peeled but left whole)
1 carrot
1 small celery stick
6 garlic cloves
4 field mushrooms
1kg beef (ox cheek, skirt/ bavette, shin, stewing steak or Jacob's ladder), chopped into 3cm cubes
6 pinches of sea salt flakes
70ml vegetable oil
a dozen black peppercorns
2 tablespoons plain flour
300ml water
1 bouquet garni (a few parsley stalks, 6 bay leaves, 3 thyme sprigs, 1 tarragon sprig – tied together with string)

To finish
1 teaspoon caster sugar (optional)
a small handful of flat-leaf parsley (optional)

Preheat the oven to 120°C/100°C fan/gas ½.

TO PREPARE Pour the red wine into a casserole dish or large saucepan and, over a high heat, cook it for 10–12 minutes (it will reduce by about a third, intensifying the flavours and colour). While the wine boils, prepare the vegetables. Peel and coarsely chop the onion, carrot and celery. Peel the garlic cloves, but leave them whole. Coarsely chop the mushrooms and keep them to one side.

Season the beef with the salt. Over a high heat, and in a heavy-based casserole dish, heat half of the oil until there's a light haze above the pan, and then sear and colour half of the diced beef for 2–3 minutes, or so. (Before searing the meat, the heat must be high. Too low, and the meat will be stewed rather than browned.) Use a slotted spoon to remove the pieces of beef and transfer them to a bowl. Sear and colour the remaining beef in two more batches and transfer it to the bowl.

Now add to the hot pan the onion, carrot, celery, garlic and peppercorns and more oil, if necessary, and cook for about 5 minutes, until lightly coloured. Add the flour and stir for a minute. Little by little, pour in the reduced wine, stirring to incorporate the flour and thicken the sauce. Pour in the water, bring to the boil, and use a slotted spoon to skim away any impurities.

Now return the beef to the casserole dish with the vegetables, and add the chopped mushrooms and the bouquet garni. Cover with a lid and transfer to the oven to cook for 3 hours. (With the oven at 120°C, the temperature in the dish is 85–90°C/185–195°F – ideal for slow cooking.)

Taste and correct the seasoning with a little caster sugar and black pepper, if necessary, rounding the sauce and giving it a final flourish. Chop the parsley and, at the table, sprinkle it over the piping-hot casserole.

Pithivier

PREP 20 MINS / COOK I HOUR 20 MINS / CHILL 50 MINS

With its glazed, golden dome of curves, the pithivier has to be one of the world's most handsome and tempting pastries. See it, and you want to slice into it. The pithivier takes its name from the French town of Pithiviers, where it originated, and the filling can be sweet or savoury. For this recipe, the puff pastry conceals a filling of slowly cooked onion and sautéed bacon lardons.

SERVES 6

plain flour, for dusting
2 sheets of all-butter
   ready-rolled puff pastry
2 egg yolks (preferably
   organic or free-range)

For the filling
3 large onions
3 garlic cloves
150g smoked streaky
   bacon
20g unsalted butter, plus
   extra for greasing the
   stone or tray
4 pinches of sea salt flakes
2 turns of ground
   black pepper
2 pinches of caraway seeds

TO PREPARE Halve the onions and finely dice them. Finely slice the peeled garlic cloves. Finely slice the bacon into lardons.

In a large sauté pan and on a medium heat, melt the butter, add the diced onion and garlic and cover with a lid. Sweeten the onion in the butter for about 10 minutes, without colouring them. Reduce the heat to low and cook for a further 15 minutes, stirring occasionally, until they are slightly browned. Season with the salt, pepper and caraway seeds. Transfer the onion to a bowl and leave to cool.

Meanwhile, place the lardons in a dry frying pan on a low–medium heat, and gently sauté them for 3–4 minutes, or until they are slightly browned. Strain the lardons through a sieve, and discard the leftover fat. Now, mix with the cooled onion and refrigerate for 20 minutes while you prepare the pastry.

On a floured surfaced, using metal rings or plates as guides, cut out a 20cm round from one pastry sheet for the base of the pithivier. Next, cut a 22cm round from the other pastry sheet – this is for the top.

Spoon the onion and bacon mix onto the centre of the puff pastry base. Using a palette knife, spread the mix evenly over the pastry, leaving a clear space of 2cm around the edge.

Beat the egg yolks and brush the egg wash around the pastry rim. Drape the other puff pastry circle neatly over the onion and bacon mixture. With your thumb, press the pastry edges gently together to seal them. Cover loosely with a sheet of greaseproof paper and refrigerate or freeze for 30 minutes to firm up the pastry.

Preheat the oven to 180°C/160°C fan/gas 4 and on the floor of the oven, place a greased baking stone, thick metal tray or upturned baking tray.

Brush the pithivier with the beaten egg. Now, using the back of a knife, score a spiral of curved lines, from the centre of the pithivier right to the edge. Carefully slide the pithivier onto the preheated baking stone or tray in the oven and bake for 45 minutes, or until the pastry is crisp and golden brown. Carefully lift the pithivier onto a wire rack and leave to rest for about 5 minutes before serving.

Pan-fried Chicken Breast, Morel Sauce

PREP 10 MINS / COOK 25 MINS / SOAKING OVERNIGHT

This great classic of French cuisine originates from my own region. I urge you to cook it for your friends, as part of a special lunch or dinner. Dried morels are best soaked overnight in cold water, and need to be washed a few times in fresh water to ensure they are thoroughly cleaned.

SERVES 2

30g dried morels
250ml cold water
a couple of handfuls of
 firm button mushrooms
 (about 180g)
2 skinless chicken breast
 fillets (each approx.
 180g), mini fillet
 removed
sea salt and black pepper
1 tablespoon unsalted
 butter
1 small glass (120ml) dry
 white wine (from Jura
 is best) or dry sherry
300ml double cream

For the leeks
1 leek
100ml water
pinch of sea salt
1 teaspoon unsalted
 butter

TO PREPARE Soak the morels in the water, ideally overnight. The following day, drain them in a colander, reserving the soaking liquor. Gently squeeze the morels to extract as much of the morel water as possible. Pass the morel liquor through a fine sieve (ideally lined with muslin) and reserve about 100ml of liquor for the sauce. Wash the morels in a colander under cold running water to remove any sand and grit. Chop the larger morels; set aside.

Wash the button mushrooms briskly in a bowl of cold water just for 10–15 seconds, drain and pat dry with kitchen paper. Halve or quarter them according to size, and keep them to one side.

Prepare the leek – this can be done a good hour before. Remove the outside two layers of the leek. Chop the leek into 2cm pieces and reserve.

Pour the water into a saucepan, place the chopped leek in the pan and add the salt and butter. Cover with a lid, and put to one side to be cooked at the last moment, when you are close to serving.

Season the chicken breast fillets with salt and pepper. In a large frying pan, melt the butter over a medium heat and, when it stops foaming, add the chicken breasts and colour lightly for 3 minutes on each side. Remove the fillets from the pan and reserve on a plate, covered with foil.

Next, the morel sauce. In the same frying pan, soften the soaked morels and button mushrooms for 1–2 minutes. Pour in the wine or sherry and bring to the boil for about 30 seconds. Then add the morel water, cream and a pinch of salt, and bring to the boil for 1–2 minutes.

Return the chicken breasts and the juices to the pan. Now lower the heat to the gentlest simmer, partly covering the pan with a lid to allow some of the steam to escape, and cook for 10–12 minutes, until cooked through. The sauce should be thick enough to coat the back of a spoon.

About 5 minutes before serving, put the pan with the chopped leek on a high heat – covered with the lid – and cook until tender.

With a slotted spoon, lift the leeks from their liquor and arrange them on warmed plates. Sit the chicken breasts on top and pour the morel sauce around the outside.

'Our lives are much improved by sharing food cultures, which doesn't stop us from keeping our own.'

VEGETABLE
DISHES

Roasted Peppers
and Freekeh
204

Griddled Summer
Vegetables
207

Pickled Radicchio
and Chicory
208

Croûte aux Morilles
211

Vegetable Kadai
212

Miso Aubergine
with Couscous
215

Cauliflower and Red Lentil Dhal

PREP 10 MINS / COOK 30 MINS

Spicy, warming and nourishing, dhal is no trouble to make, and the red lentils cook quickly. The dhal can be frozen in batches. Serve with rice.

SERVES AT LEAST 4

¼ small cauliflower
1 carrot
1 large celery stick
¼ fennel bulb
1 small onion
2 garlic cloves
2cm piece of fresh
   root ginger
25g unsalted butter
1 heaped teaspoon
   curry powder
6 curry leaves
70g red lentils
2 very generous pinches
   of sea salt flakes
generous pinch of
   cayenne pepper
450ml recently boiled
   water

To finish
sea salt flakes
juice of ½ lime

TO PREPARE Coarsely chop the cauliflower. Finely dice the carrot and celery. Dice the fennel. Finely slice the onion. Finely slice the peeled garlic. Grate or finely slice the peeled ginger.

Place a large saucepan on a medium heat, add the butter, let it melt and foam and now add the onion. Stir, cover with a lid, and cook for a couple of minutes, until the onion has softened, stirring once or twice.

Lift the lid, add the garlic, ginger, curry powder and curry leaves, and increase the heat to high. Replace the lid and cook for a further 1–2 minutes, stirring once or twice to prevent the ingredients sticking to the pan.

Reduce the heat to medium and add the cauliflower, carrot, celery and fennel, as well as the lentils, salt and cayenne. Stir well and cook for a further 2–3 minutes, stirring occasionally to prevent sticking. Add the water, stir and bring to the boil, then reduce the heat to low–medium. Continue to simmer for 20 minutes, then remove the pan from the heat.

Transfer half the dhal to a liquidiser or use a stick blender and blend it to a smooth purée. Pour this purée into the dhal in the saucepan and stir well. Taste and balance the seasoning with salt and the sharpness of the lime juice. Serve hot from the pot at the table.

OPTIONAL GARNISHES
Dress your dhal with any of these garnishes that, either together or on their own, complement many spicy dishes: nuts, seeds and spices (such as flaked almonds, sesame seeds, black onion seeds, cumin, coriander or fenugreek) toasted in a dry pan until browned to your liking; a spoonful of natural yoghurt, soured cream or buttermilk; pomegranate seeds; sliced chilli; banana shallots, sliced, tossed in flour and shallow-fried in sunflower or vegetable oil until golden and then patted dry with kitchen paper.

VARIATIONS

• Add herbs of your choice or spinach or Swiss chard leaves. Add extra richness by using coconut milk or almond milk in place of the water.

• Transform the dhal into a soup by blending it in a liquidiser and thinning it with water or coconut milk.

A Quick Ratatouille

PREP 5 MINS / COOK 15 MINS

What comes first into your mind? Is it the hero of the movie, *Ratatouille*? Or is it that dish, an iconic melting pot of vegetables, basil and garlic? Just the sound of the word takes me to Nice, where the dish is said to have originated. Nice once belonged to Italy, home of the tomato sauce, and still seems half-Italian. Traditionally, this dish is a slow-cooked, gentle infusion of flavours. The virtue of my ratatouille is that it's quick to make. The vegetables are chopped in pieces that are large enough to add plenty of texture. Ratatouille is delightful served hot or at room temperature, and wonderful if made a day in advance and then reheated for a summery lunch or supper. Make your ratatouille even more special by adding flakes of pan-fried cod on top before serving.

SERVES 4–6

1 white onion
6 garlic cloves
1 large courgette
1 aubergine
1 red pepper
4 big, fat ripe tomatoes
  (as a true Frenchman,
  I like the Marmande
  variety for this dish)
8 tablespoons extra-
  virgin olive oil
4 thyme sprigs
1 rosemary sprig
4 pinches of sea salt flakes
6–8 turns of ground
  black pepper

TO PREPARE Dice the onion, finely slice the peeled garlic and put these to one side. Halve the courgette and aubergine lengthways and chop them into 2–3cm pieces. Halve the pepper lengthways, remove the seeds and dice, again to about 2cm. Chop the tomatoes into larger chunks – size matters here as these larger pieces really do add juice, colour, texture and huge flavour. *Voilà!* The preparation is done.

Pour the olive oil into a large saucepan or casserole dish on a low heat. Let the oil heat up for a moment before adding the onion and garlic, thyme and rosemary. Gently sweat the onion and garlic in the herbs for 3–4 minutes – stir, but don't brown them.

Increase the heat to high and add the courgette, aubergine, pepper and tomato. In they go! Season with the salt and pepper and stir. Place a lid on the pan, reduce the heat to medium, and cook for 6–8 minutes, letting the vegetables steam in their own fantastic juices. Stir once or twice.

Finally, taste and correct the seasoning. Serve the ratatouille straight from the saucepan.

VARIATIONS

• The big, fat ripe tomatoes can be replaced with small ripe cherry tomatoes, which should be halved, but leave the smallest ones whole.

• Try the ratatouille with different herbs, such as marjoram or basil, or intensify the flavours with a couple of pinches of caraway, cumin or fennel seeds (for even more flavour, toast the seeds in a dry pan and then grind them).

• For luxuriance, simply add 1 tablespoon tomato purée or 100g tomato passata at the same time as the courgette, aubergine and red pepper.

My love for
COURGETTES

Casting my mind back to the mid-1980s, the courgette was quite new to Britain. This cucumber's cousin, which is known in many parts of the world as zucchini, had really only gained popularity a couple of decades earlier. Through her brilliant food writing, Elizabeth David had done much to encourage a nation to grow it, cook it, eat it.

And in the early days of Le Manoir, it caused arguments (based on cultural differences) with my head gardener, Albert. I saw a perfectly shaped, pale-green little courgette, magnificently crowned with a bright orange blossom. I dreamed of filling it with ratatouille, crushed peas with marjoram and mint or perhaps piping a soufflé within its blossom. To Albert, who resembled a stocky, white-haired Roman general, the courgette was more like a small marrow. Now, the tiny courgette is delicate and belongs to gastronomy, while the watery marrow is virtually tasteless (but to please Albert, I baked him a marrow filled with forcemeat).

The courgette has a special place in my heart, on my menus and in the gardens of Le Manoir. In the spring, courgettes bring me happiness because they are one of the first of the vegetables to appear. Soon, our taste trials begin, as we try each variety raw and cooked in different ways. For years, it was a courgette from Milan that triumphed. Then, more recently, I found myself in Provence and strolling through a market where I browsed the colourful, towering pyramids of fruit and vegetables on stalls. That was when I discovered a pale green courgette that, once cooked, revealed its sweet, powerful identity. I knew at that moment that the courgette from Provence was unbeatable.

When young and small, the courgette can be cooked in a matter of seconds, in a pan with a little water and olive oil. However, there is much to be said for maturity – whether you are a human being, an animal, bird or insect, or a vegetable, such as a courgette. Young is often pretty and decorative but, in the cycle of life, everything has an age when it is at its peak, at its best. So I urge you to try sizes, and you may find that the more mature, medium-sized vegetables often deliver optimum flavour and texture.

Roasted Sweet Potatoes with Lentils

PREP 5 MINS / COOK 30 MINS

I know that this vegetable dish is going to become one of your ever-reliable favourites. It features two nutrient-rich foods. First, the humble sweet potato, which is a mini medicine cabinet. This starchy root vegetable cooks faster than the potato and is a fantastic source of fibre and antioxidants (which protect the body from free radicals, the unstable molecules to blame for many chronic illnesses). Second, the lentils, which are rich in protein and iron so they help to strengthen the immune system and, it's believed, may reduce risk factors associated with heart disease. Apart from the considerable health benefits, it's a wholesome, nutritious, delicious one-pan meal.

SERVES 4 AS A SIDE OR 2 AS A MAIN

3 sweet potatoes
1 tin (about 400g) green lentils or cooked lentils (see page 294)
2 garlic cloves
2–3 tablespoons olive oil
2 generous pinches of sea salt flakes
4 turns of ground black pepper
2–3 handfuls of spinach
1–2 tablespoons red wine vinegar (or ¼ lemon, for squeezing)
a small handful of coarsely chopped flat-leaf parsley, to garnish (optional)

Preheat the oven to 180°C/160°C fan/gas 4.

TO PREPARE Peel the sweet potatoes and chop each of them into 8–10 pieces. Drain the lentils in a colander, lightly rinse under cold running water and put them to one side. Crush the peeled garlic to a paste with the back of a knife and put it aside.

Lay the sweet potato pieces in a roasting tin (or another ovenproof dish) and spoon over the oil. Sprinkle with the salt and pepper and toss the potatoes so that they are coated and glistening.

Roast the sweet potatoes in the oven for 20 minutes. Remove the tin from the oven, turn the potatoes, add the crushed garlic and return to the oven to roast for a further 5–10 minutes. The potatoes should be slightly golden on the edges – check they are just right by inserting the tip of a small kitchen knife into the largest piece.

Finally, remove the roasting tin from the oven and, while it's still hot, add the lentils and spinach. Gently toss – incorporating the lentils and spinach, but not breaking the potatoes as you mix. The lentils will warm through and the spinach will wilt a little. Finish with a dash of vinegar (or lemon juice) and the parsley, if using.

VARIATIONS

When adding the salt and pepper, you could also add a little of any of these: cumin, chilli, paprika, ground coriander, turmeric, ground ginger, caraway seeds or mustard seeds … or at the end, add a dash of Worcestershire Sauce.

Fricassée of Wild Mushrooms

PREP 15 MINS / COOK 5 MINS

Here, the wild mushroom triumphs. A couple of points to consider before you begin: one, use the freshest wild mushrooms to really capture the earthy, forest flavours; two, take your time with the preparation, but cook the mushrooms with speed, as they require only a moment or so in the hot pan. Any variety of wild mushroom can be used for this dish, as well as herbs such as tarragon, coriander and chervil. Among the best mushroom species are chanterelle, girolle, pied de mouton (sheep's foot), pied bleu (blue foot), hen of the woods, black trumpet and, of course, the glorious ceps. Wild mushrooms are not cheap, but button mushrooms or field mushrooms can be used to bulk out the fricassée.

SERVES 4

400g mixed wild
  mushrooms
2 tablespoons vinegar
  (for washing the
  mushrooms)
1 banana shallot or
  ½ white onion
2 garlic cloves
2 tomatoes (a plum
  tomato such as Roma
  is ideal)
a handful of flat-leaf
  parsley
50g unsalted butter
4 pinches of sea salt flakes
8 turns of ground
  black pepper
1 glass (150ml) dry
  white wine
1 tablespoon lemon juice

To serve
a good handful of croutons

TO PREPARE First, prepare the mushrooms. Remove any twigs and leaves, and cut away the woody base of the stems. Slice each mushroom lengthways into two or three pieces. (If you are using pied de mouton mushrooms, use a small knife to scrape off their velvety hairs.)

If using black trumpets, separate them out to wash on their own. Plunge the other mushrooms into a large bowl of cold water with the vinegar and swirl them for no more than 10 seconds. Mushrooms are great sponges and quickly soak up water, so they need only a swift wash. Drain the mushrooms and put them on a clean tea towel.

Next, prepare the following ingredients, putting each to one side as you go. Finely chop the shallot (or onion). Finely chop the peeled garlic. Quarter the tomatoes, remove the seeds and dice them. Finely chop the parsley.

Now we are ready to cook in a large frying pan. On a medium heat, melt half the butter. Add the chopped shallot and cook for about 30 seconds, just to soften but not to brown. Increase the heat to high, add all the wild mushrooms (apart from the black trumpets, if using) and the garlic. Season with the salt and pepper, pour in the wine, stir and sauté the mushrooms, cover with a lid and cook on full boil for 1 minute maximum.

Add the lemon juice, diced tomato, black trumpets, if using, and most of the chopped parsley – save enough parsley for a garnish – with the rest of the butter. Stir and cook for about 20 seconds. Taste and correct the seasoning.

Meanwhile, warm the croutons under a grill.

Serve from the pan, or in a large bowl, dividing the fricassée into four soup bowls. Scatter the croutons on top and finish with the remaining parsley.

My love for
WILD MUSHROOMS

———————

The adventures of my youth included extensive foraging expeditions into the forests, accompanied by my friend, René. Each of us carrying a huge basket, we'd head off as dawn was breaking, passing fields of cows as they slept. Hours – or even a day – later, we'd return, our baskets heavy with fungi. The shaded forest floor offered rich pickings: chanterelles, petit gris and girolles. When the time was just right, around May, René and I would go hunting for morels, which love a sandy, gritty bed in open clearings at the edge of the forest.

Many we sold to restaurants. Some, of course, went to Maman. She'd pickle them, or dry them in a slow oven. These were then kept in jars that lined the shelves of my father's cellar, and they helped to see us through the winter months. Foraging has become popular in Britain, but please be careful: some wild mushrooms are seriously toxic.

There is a debate about cleaning mushrooms, and whether or not they should be simply wiped clean and not washed. This is my advice: do wash them, but do so briskly, swishing them in a bowl of cold water for about 10 seconds. Then drain in a colander and pat dry with kitchen paper.

As for the cone-shaped morel, I believe that it is the finest mushroom in the world. Dried morels are available in supermarkets, and I prefer these to the fresh ones because their flavour is so much more intense and pronounced. Before cooking with them, dried morels are best soaked overnight, fully immersed in water. Or make a powder from the dried morels, or any other dried wild mushrooms, and then when you are rustling up a mushroom risotto or soup, add a teaspoon of the powder.

Roasted Peppers and Freekeh

PREP 10 MINS / COOK 40 MINS

SERVES 4

For the freekeh
150g freekeh
3 pinches of sea salt flakes
½ teaspoon fennel seeds
1 tablespoon pumpkin
  seeds
1 tablespoon sunflower
  seeds
2 pinches of ground cumin
2 pinches of ground
  coriander
450ml water

To finish the freekeh
2 cups of jasmine tea
2 tablespoons sultanas
a small bunch of coriander
a small bunch of flat-leaf
  parsley
2 tablespoons pine nuts
2 tablespoons flaked
  almonds
juice of ½ lemon
3 tablespoons extra-
  virgin olive oil

For the peppers
4 yellow or red peppers
1 tablespoon olive oil

To finish
a handful of baby
  lettuce leaves
2 teaspoons good-quality
  balsamic vinegar
1 heaped teaspoon
  flaked almonds
1 heaped teaspoon
  pine nuts
1 heaped teaspoon
  pumpkin seeds

Apart from tasting fabulous, this dish is also a well-packed medicine cabinet on the plate. Freekeh is a wheat that is harvested while young and green and, compared with brown rice, it has three times the amount of protein and twice the amount of fibre. Freekeh also has a low glycaemic index (around 43), which, when combined with its high fibre content, makes it a great choice for a diabetic who wants to lose weight. Freekeh is not gluten free as it's a type of wheat, so avoid this grain if you have gluten intolerance.

TO PREPARE Begin with 2 cups of jasmine tea. Place the sultanas in one cup and leave them until required. The other cup of tea is for you – you've earned it. Finely chop the coriander and parsley.

Alors! In a medium-sized saucepan, place the freekeh, salt, fennel seeds, pumpkin seeds, sunflower seeds, cumin and ground coriander. Cover with the water, bring to the boil on a high heat and then reduce to a simmer and continue to cook like this for about 20 minutes, stirring occasionally. You will know that your freekeh is cooked when it has absorbed all the water and still has a slight bite to it. Remove the pan from the heat, transfer the freekeh to a bowl and leave to cool.

Once the freekeh has cooled, add the pine nuts and flaked almonds, along with the lemon juice and olive oil. Strain the sultanas and add these too. Add the coriander and parsley and stir this mixture well. Taste and correct the seasoning if necessary. Put aside, ready to use as the stuffing for the peppers.

Preheat the oven to 170°C/150°C fan/gas 3½. Remove a thin slice from the base of each pepper so that the peppers stand upright. Slice the peppers crossways, about 1cm from the top – this gives you the pepper's 'lid'. Use a spoon to scoop out and then discard the seeds and white pith.

Spoon an equal amount of the freekeh mixture into each pepper. Pop the 'lid' on top and place the stuffed peppers on a baking tray or in an ovenproof dish. Brush each pepper all over with olive oil. Roast for 20 minutes.

To serve, arrange a few lettuce leaves in the centre of each plate and place a hot pepper on top. Drizzle with the balsamic vinegar and scatter with a few nuts and seeds. Serve immediately.

Griddled Summer Vegetables

PREP 10 MINS / COOK 20 MINS

A pure tribute to vegetables. I know that you can find these ingredients all year round in the supermarket, but this particular dish is best when the vegetables are seasonal, between June and September. In this recipe, the vegetables are cooked on a griddle pan, which I recommend investing in. The griddle chars the vegetables, producing extra flavour. Otherwise, cook them on the barbecue, in a sauté or frying pan or gently roast the vegetables in an oven preheated to 160°C/140°C fan/gas 3. They can be served with pesto or a simple dressing of olive oil and balsamic vinegar. This dish is perfect with the Spicy Chicken Paillard on page 155.

SERVES 4

1 small fennel bulb
1 small aubergine
1 courgette
1 red pepper
1 gem lettuce (or cos, radicchio or a combination of any of them)
6 tablespoons extra-virgin olive oil, plus 4 tablespoons
pinch of sea salt
2 turns of ground black pepper

To finish
2 tablespoons extra-virgin olive oil
2 tablespoons balsamic vinegar

TO PREPARE Thinly slice the fennel, aubergine and the courgette into ½cm slices using either a sharp knife or mandolin. Slice the pepper lengthways into quarters and discard the seeds. Reserve. So now most of the preparation is done.

Halve the gem lettuce and then blanch the halves for 10 seconds in a saucepan of boiling water. This will partly cook the lettuce and help stop it discolouring. Immerse the lettuce halves in cold water for a few seconds, and then gently squeeze out any water. Put them to one side.

In a large bowl, mix the fennel, aubergine, courgette and red pepper and drizzle with the 6 tablespoons of extra-virgin olive oil, the salt and pepper so that they are lightly coated.

Brush the lettuce with the 4 tablespoons of olive oil. Heat the griddle pan, giving it time to pick up some heat. Put a vegetable slice on the griddle to check it's hot enough – it must be hot enough to cook and to mark, or char, the vegetables.

Begin by cooking the lettuce and courgette, which will take about 2 minutes on each side. Next, the fennel, aubergine and red pepper will need about 3 minutes on each side. Remember, the griddle marks add so much flavour. Cook the vegetables in batches so as not to overload the pan and place the cooked vegetables onto a warm dish while you griddle the remaining vegetables. Once all the vegetables are cooked and ready to serve, finish the dish by adding a couple of dashes each of extra-virgin olive oil and balsamic vinegar. Serve the vegetables warm.

Pickled Radicchio and Chicory

PREP 5 MINS / COOK 5 MINS / PICKLE OVERNIGHT

The joy of pickled lettuces is that they pickle so quickly. They need only an overnight pickling and then they're ready to eat. These crunchy pickled leaves go extremely well with cold smoked meats, charcuterie and cheese, or on top of a chargrilled burger. Here, I have used a 1-litre Kilner jar, which makes an interesting feast for the eyes – you really want to open and eat what's inside. However, any suitable storage containers can be used, and the radicchio and chicory can be replaced by other firm lettuce varieties. This really shows you the miracle of pickling, which transforms flavour and texture and, of course, preserves our food.

MAKES I LARGE JAR

250ml red wine vinegar
250ml water
125g caster sugar
½ tablespoon sea salt flakes
8 turns of ground black pepper
2 star anise
3 thyme sprigs
I radicchio
2 yellow chicory

Pour the vinegar and water into a large saucepan. Add the sugar, salt, pepper, star anise and thyme. Place on a high heat and bring to the boil.

Remove the pan from the heat and leave it to cool to room temperature.

Chop the radicchio into eight pieces, lengthways and through the stalk. Halve each chicory lengthways and through the stalk.

Tightly pack the radicchio and chicory into a 1-litre Kilner jar. Pour the pickle liquor into the jar until the radicchio and chicory are immersed (push them down a little, if necessary).

Seal the jar and reserve in the fridge overnight before using the pickled vegetables. The pickled lettuces will keep for up to one month in the fridge before losing their texture.

Croûte aux Morilles

PREP 15 MINS / COOK 25 MINS

What a real treat from Franche-Comté! Golden puff pastry boxes (that's the 'croûte' or 'crust'), filled with morels in a creamy white wine sauce. A bottle of white from the Jura could accompany this dish.

SERVES 4

For the puff pastry case
300g all-butter puff pastry
1 medium egg
    (preferably organic
    or free-range)

For the filling
45g dried morels
300ml cold water
1 glass (about 200ml)
    dry white wine (from
    Jura, or dry sherry)
150g button mushrooms
1 large tablespoon
    unsalted butter
1 teaspoon sea salt flakes
4 turns of ground black
    pepper
200ml double cream

a handful of finely sliced
    chives, to garnish
    (optional)

TO PREPARE Soak the morels overnight in the cold water.

The following day … begin by making the puff pastry cases. Preheat the oven to 200°C/180°C fan/gas 6 with a baking tray on the middle shelf.

Roll out the cold puff pastry to 14cm x 24cm, and about ½cm deep. Now cut the sheet into four equal-sized rectangles, each 7cm x 12cm. Using a sharp knife, create a second rectangle within each pastry rectangle, cutting ½cm from the edge and only 2mm deep.

Place the cold rectangles of pastry on a sheet of baking parchment. Beat the egg and lightly brush it over the top of each piece. Slide the sheet of paper onto the preheated baking tray and bake for 18 minutes, until golden.

Remove from the oven and while the pastry boxes are still hot, slice the top off each pastry piece – this is the lid. Gently scrape out the middle of each rectangle to create a cavity. Put the pastry boxes and lids aside.

Now, make the filling. Drain the soaked morels in a colander over a bowl and gently squeeze them to extract as much of the morel water as possible. Pass the water through a fine sieve and reserve for the sauce. Wash the morels in a colander under cold running water to remove any sand and grit – morels are beautiful but they collect lots of sand. Reserve.

In a saucepan, bring the wine to the boil for 30 seconds, remove from the heat and put to one side. Wash the button mushrooms by swirling them in a bowl of cold water for 10 seconds and then draining. Chop them into halves or quarters, depending on their size – it's your call.

In a large sauté pan and over a medium heat, melt the butter and when it's foaming, add the chopped mushrooms and sauté them for a minute or so. Add the morels, season with the salt and black pepper and stir. Pour in the boiled wine and 50ml of the morel soaking juice. Add the cream, bring to the boil and then reduce until the sauce is creamy, rich and silky. Please taste but do not eat all of the sauce. Adjust the seasoning, as required.

Put the pastry boxes on a tray and warm in the oven for 3–4 minutes. Place each box on a plate and spoon the morels into the hollow of the pastry and over it. Sprinkle with chives, if using, place the pastry lid on top and serve.

Vegetable Kadai

PREP 20 MINS / COOK 30 MINS

We are proud to have a number of Indian chefs at Brasserie Blanc. One of them, Shailesh Kumar Jha, is an excellent chef and, very kindly, he has given me this recipe to share with you. Vegetable kadai is a flashback to his childhood in northeast India, and I am very grateful to Shailesh. The dish takes its name from the cooking utensil, a type of thick, circular and deep cooking pot, which looks like a Chinese wok. If you don't have a kadai, a wok or a large, heavy-based saucepan can be used instead. 'We ate vegetable kadai many, many times during my childhood,' says Shailesh. 'The vegetables and spices used in these dishes are cooked at high temperatures in the kadai, giving such dishes a delicious smoky flavour. Our home was filled with aromas of dry roasted spices …' *Merci*, Shailesh.

SERVES 4

Spices for the kadai masala
1 tablespoon coriander seeds (dhania)
1 tablespoon white sesame seeds (til)
1 tablespoon cumin seeds (jeera)
2 cardamom pods (elaichi)
1 cinnamon stick (dalchini)
4–6 dried red chillies

For the gravy (or sauce)
2 medium-sized potatoes
1 carrot
6–7 French beans
1 small red pepper
1 onion
4 garlic cloves
10g piece of fresh root ginger
4 tablespoons vegetable (or mustard) oil
100g cauliflower florets
1 tin (400g) chopped tomatoes (or 4 tomatoes, finely sliced)
1 teaspoon salt, or to taste
½ teaspoon ground turmeric (haldi)
½ teaspoon sugar
a handful of chopped coriander, to garnish

TO PREPARE Peel and roughly chop the potatoes and carrot, halve the French beans and slice the pepper. Finely chop the onion, peeled garlic and ginger.

Begin by preparing the kadai masala, or dry-roasted spices. Put the coriander seeds, sesame seeds, cumin seeds, cardamom, cinnamon stick and dried red chillies in a pan. Roast these over a low–medium heat for 5 minutes. The coriander seeds will start to change colour slightly and give off a strong aroma. Transfer the roasted spices to a grinder or to a mortar and pestle and grind them into powder. Set this spice powder aside.

Heat half the oil in a kadai (or a Chinese wok or deep-sided sauté pan). Add the potato and carrot and, over a medium heat, sauté them for 3–4 minutes. Add the beans and cauliflower and sauté for a further 2–3 minutes. Add the sliced pepper.

Now add the spices, stir well, and sauté for a further 2–3 minutes. Remove the pan from the heat and set the vegetables aside on a plate.

For the kadai gravy, heat the remaining oil in the same kadai, add the onion, garlic and ginger and sauté for 5–6 minutes on a medium heat, or until they start to turn golden brown.

Add the tomatoes to the pan, as well as some salt and ground turmeric. Pour in a cup of water, add the sugar – to balance the flavour of the gravy – and mix well.

Finally, add the sautéed vegetables to the gravy, stir and cook for 4–5 minutes – the gravy will thicken. Sprinkle over the coriander. Your vegetable kadai is ready. Serve it hot with Fast Flatbreads (see page 52), roti, naan or Boiled Rice (see page 292).

Miso Aubergine with Couscous

PREP 5 MINS / COOK 30 MINS

The miso is salty-sweet, the harissa brings fiery spice and, with its creaminess, the aubergine tempers the heat. The aubergine also acts as a little cooking pot for the miso and harissa. Along with the couscous, a bowl of yoghurt blended with chopped coriander is a delicious accompaniment, should you wish. The aubergine can be cooked well in advance, then brushed with the glaze and finished in the oven shortly before serving.

SERVES 4

2 medium-sized
  aubergines
20g miso paste (I like
  brown rice miso)
20g rose harissa
1 teaspoon honey
  (or maple syrup)
1 teaspoon sesame oil
1 teaspoon ground cumin
2 tablespoons extra-
  virgin olive oil
4 pinches of sea salt flakes
juice of ¼ lemon
2 tablespoons vegetable
  oil, for frying

For the couscous
100g piquillo peppers
8 coriander sprigs
150ml water
100g couscous
60g sultanas
40g flaked almonds
60ml extra-virgin olive oil
juice of ½ lemon
sea salt flakes and
  black pepper

Preheat the oven to 180°C/160°C fan/gas 4.

TO PREPARE Slice the aubergines in half lengthways, and lightly score the flesh side in a criss-cross pattern. Dice the piquillo peppers and coarsely chop the coriander.

In a small bowl, make the marinade by mixing the miso, harissa, honey, sesame oil and ground cumin.

Brush the aubergine flesh with the olive oil, season it with the salt and rub in the lemon juice.

Heat the vegetable oil in a large frying pan over a high heat. Lay the aubergine halves in the pan, flesh-side down, and cook for 1 minute, until golden. Turn the aubergines and continue to cook for 3–5 minutes. Remove the pan from the heat.

Brush the miso-harissa glaze onto the flesh side of the aubergines and transfer them to the oven for 10–15 minutes, until the flesh is cooked.

Now the couscous, which can be made while the aubergines are cooking in the oven. In a small pan, bring the water to the boil and add the couscous. Cover with a tight-fitting lid (or non-pvc clingfilm) and leave the couscous in its own steam for 5 minutes, so that it absorbs the water and puffs up.

Once the water has been absorbed, stir with a fork and add the piquillo peppers, sultanas and flaked almonds. Pour in the olive oil and the juice of the lemon half. Add the chopped coriander and season to your taste with salt and pepper.

To serve, spoon couscous into the middle of each plate and top with the miso aubergine, drizzling over any cooking juices.

'Master the craft of growing flavours. Begin with just a little salt – you can always add more. Next, a few turns of pepper or a pinch of spice, and lastly a little lemon or a pinch of sugar. Keep tasting as you go.'

CELEBRATIONS

Gravadlax
221

Glazed Ham
222

Roast Rib of Beef
225

Slow-roasted Shoulder
of Lamb, Harissa
226

Roast Celeriac Fondants,
Celeriac Jus
228

Celeriac Tatin or Pie
229

Gravadlax

PREP 20 MINS / CURE 24 HOURS, FREEZE 1–1½ HOURS, CHILL 2 HOURS ... the wait is worth it

A classic of Scandinavian origin, gravadlax epitomises the art of curing. The best-available fresh salmon is pressed with a mix of seasonings, dill and lemon zest. The rest is left mostly to Mother Nature's ever-dependable cooking tool – time. It can be a special snack on a slice of rye bread, a starter for a lunch or dinner party or a Christmastime treat. The gravadlax and cucumber can be prepared a day ahead or the salmon can be cured and then kept in the freezer until the slicing stage. This recipe is a long-time favourite in the Brasserie Blanc restaurants.

SERVES 6–8

½ bunch (about 10g) of dill, plus 1 small bunch (about 20g) to finish the salmon
½ lemon
20g sea salt flakes
15g caster sugar
½ teaspoon ground white pepper
500g salmon, skinless and pin boned
1 heaped teaspoon Dijon mustard

For the cucumber salad
1 cucumber
4 large pinches of sea salt flakes
2 large pinches of ground white pepper
2 tablespoons white wine vinegar
2 dill sprigs, leaves picked
2 tablespoons soured cream (optional, but it will add a little extra luxury)

TO PREPARE Line a baking tray (or roasting tin) with non-pvc clingfilm – enough to wrap the salmon. Finely chop the dill and zest the lemon.

In a bowl, mix the ½ bunch of dill and the lemon zest with the salt, sugar and white pepper. Sprinkle half this mixture along the centre of the clingfilm, and then place the salmon on top. Now cover the top of the salmon with the rest of the salt mixture, so that both sides of the fish are evenly covered.

Tightly wrap the clingfilm around the salmon and refrigerate for 24 hours. During this time, the salt mixture extracts the water content from the salmon, creating a wonderful exchange of flavours as the fish is cured. After 24 hours, place the salmon under cold running water to wash away the salt mixture. Pat the salmon dry with kitchen paper.

Next (and I'll let you into a little chef secret), to achieve perfect slices, wrap the salmon in clingfilm once again and transfer to the freezer for 1–1½ hours (or until required). Now it is firm enough to slice perfectly.

Place the salmon on a chopping board and, using a sharp, thin-bladed knife, cut slices, each about ½cm thick, not all the way through so as to keep the salmon in one piece. To finish, place the salmon on a board lined with clingfilm, leaving an overlap large enough to wrap around the fish. Brush the mustard over the salmon, then scatter over the remaining bunch of finely chopped dill. Wrap the fish tightly in the clingfilm and press the mustard-dill coating firmly into the salmon. Refrigerate for at least 2 hours, so that it has thawed.

For the cucumber salad, peel the cucumber, halve it lengthways, remove the seeds and slice very finely into ribbons (use a mandolin with a spaghetti attachment, a spiralizer or simply a sharp knife). These strips should be just long enough to wrap around a fork. Add the salt and leave for a minimum of 10 minutes. Drain off the liquid and add the white pepper and vinegar. Before serving, stir in the dill and soured cream, if using.

Serve the salmon, sliced through, on individual plates or, for a more celebratory touch, place the salmon and cucumber on a large serving dish.

Glazed Ham

PREP 10 MINS / COOK 2½ HOURS, PLUS 40 MINS TO CARAMELISE

SERVES AT LEAST 12–14

1 large onion

1 carrot

½ stick of celery

3 garlic cloves

1 bay leaf

2 thyme sprigs

1 curly or flat-leaf parsley sprig

1 teaspoon black peppercorns

3.5kg gammon, on the bone

3–4 litres recently boiled water

For the glaze

3 teaspoons English mustard

60ml dark rum

2 teaspoons mixed spice

1 teaspoon ground coriander

¼ teaspoon ground cloves

2–3 turns of ground black pepper

80g runny honey

40g Demerara sugar

Cooking times for varying sizes of gammon:

8kg gammon on the bone – 6½ hours

5kg gammon on the bone – 3 hours

2.5kg gammon on the bone – 2 hours

Each of these hams requires an additional 40 minutes to caramelise in the oven.

A much-loved symbol of Christmas, glazed ham says party, celebration and indulgence. On a large board, and with a sharpened carving knife beside it, the ham is an irresistible temptation. My recipe requires a deep roasting tin, rather than a massive stockpot, thereby sparing the windows in your home from being steamed up. Gammon, incidentally, is the raw cut of meat. Once cooked, it is ham.

Preheat the oven to 150°C/130°C fan/gas 2.

TO PREPARE Coarsely chop the onion, carrot (just wash it, no need to peel), celery and peeled garlic. Put them into a large, deep roasting tin as you go.

Spread the vegetables evenly in the tin and add the bay leaf, thyme sprigs, parsley sprig and black peppercorns. Sit the gammon on top of the chopped vegetables and herbs. Pour in the recently boiled water so that it comes about two-thirds up the side of the tin. Loosely cover with tinfoil. Very carefully transfer the tin to the oven (if you prefer, you can add the hot water when the tin is in the oven). Cook for 2½ hours.

Remove the roasting tin from the oven – be careful of the hot water and steam as you open the oven door. Leave the oven on, as soon you will be glazing the ham. Leave the ham to cool slightly before transferring it to a shallower roasting tin (or a baking tray). Strain the cooking liquor, and leave this to cool. (It can be stored in the fridge or freezer and used for other dishes or as a base for soups.)

When the ham is cool enough to touch, remove the skin but try to keep as much fat as possible (if necessary, use a sharp knife or a spoon to help separate the skin if it sticks to the fat). The fat has a lot of flavour, and will help give a lovely crust.

To glaze the ham, mix the mustard with the rum to form a smooth paste. Add the mixed spice, coriander, cloves, finely ground black pepper, honey and Demerara sugar. Lightly brush the paste all over the ham.

Transfer the ham to the oven for 40 minutes, basting it several times until it is deep-amber in colour. Allow the ham to cool for at least 30 minutes before carving, although of course it's irresistible when it's warm. Practise your carving skills, and let the celebrations commence! *Joyeux Noël!*

Roast Rib of Beef

PREP 10 MINS / COOK 2 HOURS / REST AT LEAST 30 MINS AND UP TO 2 HOURS

You are the lunch guest. The front door is opened and, as you step inside, you are greeted by the most delicious aromas that set your nose twitching. 'Something smells fantastic.' You make your way towards the kitchen. There it is – a mighty and spectacular roasted rib of beef, recently removed from the oven and resting on a board beneath a loose covering of tinfoil. The pop of a cork completes the scene. Rib of beef is an occasional, memorable treat. Sometimes a bit of splashing out is required, and you will do well to buy the best-quality beef, which has been hung for at least 20 days so that it's perfectly tender. A red wine sauce is a fabulous accompaniment (see page 290), and can be made a day or two in advance. Allow a chilled rib of beef at least 5 hours to come to room temperature before cooking, or remove it from the fridge the night before cooking. As an accompaniment, I strongly recommend Adam's renowned ruffled, roasted potatoes (see page 234). Steamed French beans or broccoli are also a natural accompaniment, cooked at the last moment to retain taste, colour and nutrients.

SERVES AT LEAST 6 GUESTS

1 carrot
1 onion
an aged 3-bone rib of beef (3–3.5kg), at room temperature
sea salt flakes and black pepper
800ml recently boiled water

Preheat the oven to 170°C/150°C fan/gas 3½.

TO PREPARE Coarsely chop the carrot (just wash it, no need to peel) and the onion.

Scatter the carrot and onion into a roasting tin, along with any beef trimmings. Use a sharp knife to score the beef fat in a criss-cross pattern. Rub salt and pepper into both sides, and into the fat. Place the joint on top of the chopped carrot and onion.

Roast for 30 minutes, and soon the most wonderful aromas begin to fill your home. Now, remove the tin from the oven and pour in the water. Return the rib in its tin to the oven, and continue to roast for 1½ hours. So it has a total of 2 hours in the oven. If using a digital thermometer, insert the probe into the centre of the beef and follow these temperatures as a guide: 50°C for rare; 55°C for medium rare; 60°C for medium; 65°C medium-well done.

When you have removed the beef from the oven, loosely cover it with tinfoil. Leave it to rest for at least 30 minutes and for up to 2 hours. Yes, up to 2 hours. One of your anxious guests will say, 'Why are you leaving it so long? It will go cold.' Reassure them. You are in full control, and know what you are doing. Resting is crucial and enables the juices to redistribute themselves within this large and majestic piece of meat – ultimately, resting equals succulence.

Carve with care in front of your guests, using a well-sharpened knife. Serve with accompaniments, including Adam's renowned roasties and the red wine sauce. Then sit back and relish the applause.

Slow-roasted Shoulder of Lamb, Harissa

PREP 10 MINS / COOK ABOUT 4½ HOURS / MARINATE 1 HOUR (BUT NOT ESSENTIAL)

When I was about 12 years old, I was introduced to the food of Algeria, and by strange means. This was during the Algerian War, and in France there were camps for Algerian refugees. One such camp was close to my village and, with my friend René, I would go and visit these intriguing, kind and friendly people. They fed us well. I remember seeing whole lambs roasted on the spit and, as the meat was turned, it was also painted with the spicy juices. For my young palate, it was perhaps a bit too spicy. I was the stranger who was drawn in, and have never forgotten their kindness. This dish does not require a whole lamb. When it comes to slow cooking lamb, the shoulder is the best cut, meltingly tender and incredibly tasty. When harissa is added, this is a wonderful dish, and the chickpeas will only complement it. A shoulder of lamb varies in weight, becoming heavier as the year progresses. A 2.5kg shoulder, like the one in this recipe, will take about 4½ hours; one weighing 3kg will need 5½ hours. Aim to remove it from the fridge 4–5 hours before cooking to come to room temperature.

SERVES 4–6

1 tablespoon sea salt
1 tablespoon ground cumin
100g rose harissa
100ml extra-virgin olive oil
2.5kg new season's
  shoulder of lamb
300ml water

For the chickpea salad
1 jar (230g) piquillo
  peppers
2 preserved beldi lemons
a large handful of curly or
  flat-leaf parsley
2 tins (each 400g) chickpeas
sea salt and black pepper

VARIATIONS

• Any cut of lamb can be
  cooked in the same way.

• The lamb may be
  served with lentils,
  couscous, roasted
  squash or aubergine.

TO PREPARE Mix together the salt, cumin and harissa, and then add the extra-virgin olive oil. Place the lamb in a roasting tin. Lightly score the skin of the lamb and rub it all over with the salty harissa mixture. At this point, you can leave the lamb for an hour, allowing the harissa flavours to infuse, but this is not essential.

Preheat the oven to 180°C/160°C fan/gas 4.

Roast the lamb for 20 minutes, and then reduce the temperature to 150°C/130°C fan/gas 2. Cover the lamb shoulder loosely with foil, and return it to the oven to roast for a further 2 hours.

Now baste the lamb, add the water and return it to the oven for 2 hours, again loosely covered with foil.

While the lamb is roasting, chop the piquillo peppers, finely chop the preserved lemons (skin and pulp) and coarsely chop the parsley. Put them to one side; you will need them to finish the dish.

Remove the lamb from the oven. Spoon out most of the fat from the tin, leaving the roasting juices. To the warm roasting juices, add the chickpeas, peppers and lemon. Add the parsley too and season with the salt and pepper. Toss together and bring to the boil on the hob. Place the lamb shoulder on a platter with the chickpea salad.

Bring the lamb to the table and invite your guests to help themselves. The lamb will be tender enough to fall from the bone with a spoon, though it can be carved if you prefer.

Roast Celeriac Fondants, Celeriac Jus

PREP 40 MINS / COOK 1 HOUR

SERVES 2

*For the roasted
celeriac fondants*
about 400g celeriac
   (after trimming the
   celeriac for the jus)
40g unsalted butter
3 thyme sprigs
1 rosemary sprig
50ml water

For the celeriac jus
1 garlic clove
4 tablespoons sunflower
   or vegetable oil
40g unsalted butter
200ml Madeira
200ml water, plus the
   cooking liquor from
   the celeriac
2 thyme sprigs
1 rosemary sprig
a few celeriac leaves
   or celery leaves, if you
   have them
1 teaspoon cornflour
   (or arrowroot)
2–3 tablespoons water

*For the steamed
chicory and kale*
1 yellow chicory
2–3 handfuls of kale
100ml water
20g unsalted butter
2 pinches of sea salt flakes
ground black pepper

1 tablespoon walnut or
   hazelnut oil, to garnish

Going back many years, I created this dish at Le Manoir as I wanted to give a truly wonderful meal to our vegetarian guests. All the elements of the dish can be prepared one day in advance, and reheated when required.

TO PREPARE Halve the chicory lengthways and separate it into its leaves. Remove the roots and slice away the top and base of the celeriac so that it stands upright, making it easier to then peel. Coarsely chop up all these trimmings (the roots, peelings, top and base) for the celeriac jus and put them aside. Finely slice the peeled garlic. Reserve.

The chicory and kale can be prepared in advance, and then cooked just before serving. Pour the water into a pan and lay the chicory and kale on top. Add the butter, salt and pepper. Cover with a lid, and leave.

To make the jus, in a large sauté pan over a high heat, sauté the celeriac trimmings in the oil for 1–2 minutes until golden. Reduce the heat to medium–high, add the butter, and cook until a rich, dark brown.

Pour the Madeira into the hot pan and leave it to reduce by half. Next, pour in the water and add the thyme, rosemary and garlic. Bring it back to the boil, then reduce to a gentle simmer and cook like this for 10 minutes.

If you have celeriac or celery leaves, chop them finely, add and cook for a further 2 minutes to give a peppery burst to the sauce. To thicken the sauce, mix the cornflour with a couple of tablespoons of water, and stir this into the jus. Preheat the oven to 170°C/150°C fan/gas 3½.

The remaining piece of celeriac is now cut crossways. This gives you two large discs, or fondants, each about 3cm deep. Use a cutter, about 8–10cm in diameter, to cut the discs neatly. In a large ovenproof sauté pan, and over a medium heat, melt the butter and when it stops foaming, add the discs and cook for 10 minutes on each side, until beautifully dark brown. Season, add the thyme, rosemary and water, cover loosely with foil and transfer to the oven to cook for 15 minutes.

When the celeriac has been in the oven for 10 minutes, put the chicory and kale on a medium–high heat for 4–5 minutes. Meanwhile, reheat the jus.

To dress each plate, place a celeriac fondant in the centre of the plate with the darkest side facing you. Arrange the chicory and kale around it and pour the jus over. Drizzle with the walnut or hazelnut oil to finish.

Celeriac Tatin or Pie

PREP 5 MINS / COOK 30 MINS

This is an interesting take on the roast celeriac recipe, and the only extra ingredient is puff pastry. Rich, buttery and flaky, the pastry adds a new dimension, transforming it into a dish that's really moreish. With the puff pastry, you can choose to make either a pie or a Tatin, depending on the mood that you're in. I like to celebrate both. Serve with steamed chicory and kale (see opposite).

NOTE: Before making this dish, an important tip: the celeriac needs to be cooled to room temperature, and the sheet of puff pastry should be chilled to make it easy to handle and wrap.

SERVES 2

2 Roast Celeriac
  Fondants (see opposite)
1 packet all-butter
  ready-rolled puff pastry
1 egg yolk (preferably
  organic or free-range)
Celeriac Jus (see opposite)

Preheat the oven to 180°C/160°C fan/gas 4.

Cut two circles of chilled puff pastry that are wide enough to wrap completely over the top and sides of each celeriac fondant.

Place the celeriac fondants onto a non-stick baking tray, darkest-side up. Drape the cold puff pastry around the celeriac, and tuck it in with the back of a knife or the handle of a teaspoon, creating a pattern on the base of the pastry.

Stir the egg yolk with a pastry brush and brush this all over the pastry (in the hot oven, the egg wash will give a beautiful golden crust). With a small knife, make a hole in the middle of the pastry.

Bake for 30 minutes, or until the pastry is golden and crisp.

Remove the tray from the oven. Transfer each celeriac to the plates, either as a pie with the pastry on top, or turn it over, with the pastry underneath – a nod to the Tatin sisters who created this concept. Either way, it will be heavenly.

Pour the hot jus around the plate and serve with the steamed chicory and kale.

'The simple celeriac fondant,
left, can be easily transformed into
a tempting Tatin or pie, below.'

Leftover Turkey Curry

PREP 10 MINS / COOK 30 MINS

Post-Christmas is not always nice. There are some good memories, but a certain sense of sadness that it didn't last forever. But don't be so gloomy. There is still meat on the turkey, and it can be used to great effect in this easy curry, served with basmati or brown rice, the refreshing raita to cool the heat and Fast Flatbreads (see page 52). Maybe another bottle of wine will be opened (I'd suggest a floral Riesling or Gewürztraminer). The conversation will flow once more, making the tomorrows beyond Christmas rather pleasant. The spicy heat is your call, but chillies vary in heat so I taste a little of the raw chilli before adding it to the pan. The base for the curry can be made in advance and stored in the freezer until required.

SERVES 4–6

1 large onion
4 garlic cloves
about 1 thumb of
   fresh root ginger
   (or 2 teaspoons
   ground ginger)
8 tomatoes (or 2 tins
   chopped tomatoes)
2 mild red chillies (such
   as Rio Grande or
   Snub Nose)
about 500g leftover
   turkey meat
50g unsalted butter
6 cardamom pods
3 cloves
1 teaspoon ground
   coriander
1 teaspoon ground cumin
10 black peppercorns
4 pinches of sea salt flakes

*For the cucumber raita
(optional)*
¼ cucumber
150g natural yoghurt
a few mint leaves,
   chopped (optional)

To finish (optional)
a few coriander leaves
sliced spring onions

TO PREPARE Finely dice the onion. Finely slice the peeled garlic. Finely slice or grate the peeled ginger. Chop the tomatoes into bite-sized pieces. Finely slice the chillies (and may I recommend washing your hands afterwards). Coarsely chop the turkey. Slice the cucumber lengthways, remove the seeds and finely dice.

In a medium-sized saucepan covered with a lid, and over a medium heat, sweat the onion in the butter for 5 minutes until soft. Remove the lid and continue to cook for a few minutes until the onion begins to brown, stirring from time to time to achieve sweetness and an even, golden colour.

Add the garlic, ginger and chilli and cook, stirring, for about 1 minute.

In a separate small frying pan, on a low heat, gently toast the spices – the cardamom, cloves, coriander, cumin and black peppercorns – for a minute. This will extract their essential oils and maximise flavour. Add the toasted spices to the onion mixture, stir well and cook for 1 minute.

Stir in the chopped tomatoes, bring to a simmer, season and taste. Reduce the heat to medium and leave this sauce to reduce and thicken slightly for a couple of minutes, so that all the flavours are infused.

Add the cooked turkey meat, cover with a lid and leave on a very low heat for about 15 minutes.

When you are ready to serve, taste and adjust the seasoning if necessary.

For the raita, mix the cucumber with the yoghurt and, if using, chopped mint.

Serve the curry with the raita, a generous helping of rice or flatbreads and garnish with coriander leaves and sliced spring onions, if you wish.

Adam's Roast Potatoes

PREP 10 MINS / COOK 55 MINS

Soon after arriving in Britain I began to notice a familiarity when my new friends discussed recipes. They talked of how they got their Yorkshire puddings to rise heavenwards. They shared recipes for the tastiest gravy and the crumbliest crumble. These topics are still aired over the Sunday roast. Few British cooks are more animated than when bragging about their 'roasties' – the magnificent golden, crispy-edged roast potatoes. As a Frenchman, I dare not brag about mine. But I implore you to try the roast potatoes made by Adam Johnson, who has worked with me and been my protégé for 17 years. His really are the best, as you will soon see. The recipe has been passed down the Johnson family line, and now to you. Tips from Adam: for crispiness, it's essential to preheat the goose fat. The potatoes must be fiercely par-boiled in well-salted water (it seems like a lot of salt, but it's to season them). Ruffling the potatoes in a colander creates hundreds of layers that'll crisp when roasted. Adam and I have found that the Lincolnshire variety of potato, fluffy and light, is the best for roasties and chips. Maris Piper or King Edward are excellent too, and easily available.

SERVES 4

1kg potatoes
2 litres water
20g sea salt flakes
200g goose or duck fat
3 rosemary sprigs
6 garlic cloves
2 pinches of sea salt
   and black pepper,
   or to taste

Preheat the oven to 200°C/180°C fan/gas 6.

TO PREPARE Peel the potatoes and cut them into halves or quarters, depending on size – a mismatch of sizes seems to please all.

In a medium saucepan on a high heat, bring the water and the salt to a boil. (This may seem like a lot of salt, but it is only to season the potatoes at this early stage.)

Add the potatoes and boil fiercely over a high heat for 8–10 minutes, or until the potato edges begin to flake.

Meanwhile, heat the goose fat in a deep roasting tin in the oven.

Drain the potatoes in a colander and leave them to stand for 2 minutes, to let the steam escape. Now shake the colander gently to make the potatoes ruffled and fluffy.

Remove the roasting tin from the oven. Carefully slide the potatoes into the hot, sizzling fat, and ensure that they are a single layer, not on top of one another. Baste the potatoes and roast them for a total of 40–45 minutes. After 20 minutes, turn the potatoes.

In the final 5 minutes of roasting, add the rosemary and garlic cloves. After the total 40–45 minutes of roasting, use a slotted spoon to transfer the potatoes to a warm bowl or serving dish and season to taste.

Serve, and allow yourself a smile as everyone talks about – and tucks into – the best roast potatoes.

Quick Carrots Vichy

PREP 5 MINS / COOK 15 MINS

This renowned dish of carrots is claimed by the good people of Vichy, the spa town that is north-west of Lyon, the belly of France. Vichy was famous for its exceptional mineral water, and there you have the connection. The carrots, you see, are cooked in just a little water and with some butter. Traditionally the carrots are cooked whole, but here is my recipe for a quick version. Quick because the carrots are finely sliced so they cook within about 15 minutes. This can be prepared an hour in advance, and then simply switch on the heat beneath the pan when the main course is almost ready to serve. Carrots Vichy are perfect with roasted meats, a Christmas feast or with Marmalade Duck (see page 156).

SERVES 4

6 carrots
1 banana shallot
 (or ½ white onion)
2 garlic cloves
a large handful of
 flat-leaf parsley
1 tablespoon unsalted
 butter
3 pinches of sea salt flakes
6 turns of ground black
 pepper
150ml water

TO PREPARE Halve the carrots lengthways and finely slice each half crossways (or use a mandolin slicer, if you have one). Finely chop the shallot (or finely dice the onion, if using). Finely slice the peeled garlic. Put the onion and garlic to one side. Coarsely chop the parsley and put to one side.

In a large sauté pan on a medium heat, melt the butter. Add the shallot and garlic and sweat them in the pan for 2–3 minutes (this will also sweeten them).

Add the carrots, season with the salt and pepper, stir and sauté – still on a medium heat – for 3–4 minutes.

Pour in the water, cover with a lid and continue to cook for 7–10 minutes. As the carrots cook, they'll release their flavours into the water, which reduces and creates the most wonderful juice. You'll have the best carrots in terms of flavour, texture, colour and nutrients.

Add the chopped parsley and, if necessary, add a tablespoon or two more water. Replace the lid and cook gently for another minute or two until the carrots are cooked and you have a delicious buttery glaze from the reduced cooking juices to pour over and serve with the carrots.

C'est tout! Taste and, if necessary, adjust the seasoning before serving.

Christmas Pudding, as Maman Loved It

PREP 20 MINS / COOK 3½–5 HOURS / REHEAT 1–2 HOURS

This recipe is a Manoir classic and, over the years, I have cherished that moment of boarding Eurostar and heading home for Christmas. Maman Blanc would greet me with, 'Have you got the Christmas pudding?' But in French, of course. Then to Christmas Day … Outside, the wind howls, huge snowflakes drift. Indoors, and after the bûche de Noël, I flambé the Christmas pudding and my family comes close to singing 'God Save the Queen'.

unsalted butter, for greasing
the pudding basin

For the pudding
1 orange
1 Bramley apple
4 tablespoons treacle
80g raisins
100g sultanas
280g candied peel, chopped
40g plain flour
70g breadcrumbs
(brown bread)
1 heaped tablespoon
ground almonds
100g muscovado sugar
100g suet (beef or
vegetable)
4 pinches of mixed spice
2 pinches of sea salt flakes
1 medium egg (preferably
organic or free-range)
2 tablespoons rum
4 tablespoons Cognac
1 tablespoon Guinness
1 tablespoon ruby port

To seal the pudding
3–4 tablespoons Cognac

To serve
Armagnac or Cognac,
to flame
Armagnac Butter
(see page 297)
or brandy butter

NOTE: The recipe makes 1 x 1-litre pudding or 2 x ½-litre puddings. This Christmas pudding can be prepared and steamed 2 months in advance, stored in a cool place and steamed again before serving.

TO PREPARE Well grease the pudding basin (or two smaller basins) with butter. Zest and juice the orange. Grate the apple. Slightly warm the treacle to loosen it.

In a large bowl, mix the orange zest and juice, grated apple and treacle with all of the remaining pudding ingredients.

Transfer the mix to the pudding basin, filling it to 1cm below the rim. Cover with a circle of greaseproof paper, followed by a large piece of foil. Tie this tight with string.

TO COOK Steam the pudding for 5 hours, or the smaller ones for 3½–4 hours. If you do not have a steamer, cook on a wire rack in a pan, or upturned plate, in simmering water, and top up the water occasionally.

Once cooked, remove the basins from the steamer and leave to cool. Unwrap, pour the Cognac over the top and rewrap in non-pvc clingfilm. Store in a cool place until needed.

TO REHEAT AND SERVE Reheat the large pudding by steaming it for about 2 hours, the smaller ones for about 1 hour. The longer you steam them, the darker they will become. Turn the puddings out onto a serving dish and decorate with some holly.

Heat a ladleful of Armagnac or Cognac over a flame. When the spirit flames, pour it over the pudding. Serve with Armagnac butter or brandy butter.

Frozen Meringue, Blackcurrant Coulis

PREP 15 MINS / COOK 45 MINS / FREEZE AT LEAST 3–4 HOURS

This recipe was inspired by the blackcurrant pavlova that we often serve at Brasserie Blanc. Then, Monsieur Benoit, of Le Manoir, created a meringue to die for. It is a barely cooked meringue dome, with a crispy crunch and an inside that's as soft as the poached meringue in Iles Flottantes. It is ice cold too, which reduces the sweetness, and the blackcurrant contrasts brilliantly with the meringue. This generous recipe makes more than enough meringues and any that are not used may be stored in the freezer. For true decadence, add a few marshmallows (see page 242).

SERVES 4–6 (MAKES 8–10 MERINGUES)

For the soft meringues
3 medium egg whites (preferably organic or free-range) (about 100g)
100g caster sugar
50g icing sugar, sifted

For the blackcurrant coulis
300g blackcurrants
2 tablespoons water
about 50g caster sugar, depending on the acidity of the fruit, plus extra caster sugar, for dusting the blackcurrants

For the Chantilly cream
150ml whipping or double cream
1 teaspoon vanilla bean paste or vanilla essence (or 1 tablespoon Vanilla Bean Purée, see page 297)

To serve
vanilla ice cream

Preheat the oven to 110°C/90°C fan/gas ¼. Line a large baking tray with greaseproof paper.

To make the meringues, in a food mixer on full power, whisk the egg whites to stiff, shiny peaks. When the eggs start to foam, add the sugar little by little. This will take about 10 minutes. Using a spatula, gently fold in the icing sugar for a few minutes, ensuring it is well incorporated.

Take a little bit of the meringue mixture and stick under each corner of the greaseproof paper to hold it in place. Now take a large tablespoonful of mixture and let it create its own architecture, spooning about 8–10 meringues onto the tray. After spooning each meringue, dip the back of the spoon into the centre, making a cradle to hold the ice cream.

Bake for 40–45 minutes to achieve a light crust. Remove the tray from the oven. Allow the meringues to cool for 5 minutes and then transfer the meringues to the freezer for at least 3–4 hours. Freezing the meringues gives a totally different eating experience, as you will taste. Beware, these meringues are extraordinarily fragile so be very careful when moving them, even when frozen. Leftover meringues can be reserved for another feast.

Now for the blackcurrant coulis, which is very easy. Take a couple of handfuls of the blackcurrants, sprinkle the water over them, mix with the extra caster sugar, and shake so they are covered with the sugar. Put to one side.

Blend the remaining blackcurrants and sugar to a purée. Pass the purée through a fine sieve, pressing well with the back of a ladle. If the purée is too thick, thin it with 1–2 tablespoons of water. Reserve.

Next, the Chantilly cream. Whip the cream so that it's foamy light, and not quite at the stage of soft peaks. Stir in the vanilla. Reserve in the fridge.

All that remains is to assemble this delicious dessert. Spoon the coulis in a circle around the outside of the plate. Place the meringue in the centre, then place a scoop of ice cream in the meringue's cradle. Add the Chantilly cream and a little more coulis, perhaps. Dot the plate with the sugar-coated blackcurrants and add a few of the irresistible marshmallows, if using.

Blackcurrant Marshmallows

PREP SET ASIDE AN HOUR TO MAKE / COOK 10 MINS / SET 1 HOUR / FREEZE 3 HOURS

I have long had a fascination for two of the world's favourite treats: popcorn and marshmallow. That's mostly because I had never made them and was intrigued by their mysteries. This book inspired me. Before you begin, I must say this is not so simple, yet it's rewarding to make the most colourful of guilty pleasures. They can be a gift for a friend, or a tantalising, plump decoration for desserts – such as for my dish of Frozen Meringue, Blackcurrant Coulis (see page 240).

MAKES ABOUT 80 BITE-SIZED MARSHMALLOWS

9 gelatine leaves

350g blackcurrants, fresh or frozen

240ml water

550g caster sugar, plus 20g

2 large egg whites (preferably organic or free-range) (about 75g)

2 drops of lemon juice

100g cornflour

100g icing sugar

Soak the gelatine leaves in a bowl of cold water for at least 10 minutes.

Simmer the blackcurrants for 5 minutes in a small saucepan over medium heat, and then blend to a purée in a liquidiser or with a stick blender. Pass the purée through a sieve.

Return the purée to the saucepan and warm it through. Squeeze the excess water from the softened gelatine leaves and stir them in. Reserve in a bowl.

Pour the water into a medium (16–18cm) saucepan and then add the 550g caster sugar. Leave it for 5 minutes to absorb the sugar (not on the heat). Next, heat the sugar with the water to 115°C/240°F.

While the sugar is cooking, and in a food mixer on medium speed, whisk the egg whites with the 20g caster sugar and lemon juice to soft peaks.

In a large bowl, and using a hand whisk, whisk the cooked sugar into the blackcurrant purée. Now with a spatula, fold this into the meringue. Return the mix to the food mixer and on full power whisk until cool (37°C/100°F).

Line a baking tray (about 25cm x 33cm x 2cm deep) with non-pvc clingfilm (or a silicone mat). Pour the mixture into the tray and spread it out evenly using a palette knife. Cover with another sheet of clingfilm and leave to set for 1 hour at room temperature, then transfer the tray, covered with clingfilm, to the freezer for at least 3 hours. Freezing will make it easier to cut.

In a bowl, mix the cornflour and icing sugar. Now peel off the top layer of clingfilm (or the silicone mat) and, with a hot blade, trim the marshmallow and then cut it into bite-sized cubes. Wipe the blade with a damp cloth if the marshmallow begins to stick, and reheat.

As you cut the cubes, roll them, three or four at a time, in the cornflour and icing sugar mixture. Dust away the excess, gently shaking a few at a time between your fingers. Keep them for up to 2 weeks in a sealed jar on a kitchen shelf, but watch out for little fingers.

CHEESE

'There's a new revolution taking place
and it's not French. Sustainability and
the environment will become the
most powerful drivers of change.'

Baked Camembert
248

Cheese Fondue
251

Croque Monsieur
252

Baked Camembert

PREP 5 MINS / COOK 20 MINS

If you feel lazy but fancy a party, and if you happen to have a ripe Camembert in your fridge, then it's time to get it out. Baked cheese can be relished, like a warm mini fondue, before or after dessert. Or it can be served with drinks before supper, as a canapé to dip into and share. Or perhaps it is an indulgent snack when it's cold and rainy outside. As the cook, your challenge is not intimidating. Most of the work is done instead by the oven's heat, which melts this iconic French cheese so that – beyond the white rind – it's warm, gooey, runny and irresistible. All you need do is remove the lid of the Camembert (which is best when aged and chalky), score the snowy surface and add a combination of rosemary, garlic and chilli.

SERVES 2–4

1 rosemary sprig
2 garlic cloves
1 red chilli
1 box (about 250g)
  Camembert cheese

Preheat the oven to 180°C/160°C fan/gas 4.

TO PREPARE Pick the rosemary leaves from the sprig. Finely slice the peeled garlic and red chilli. Put to one side.

Prepare the Camembert by removing the lid of the box and partly unwrapping the cheese so that the base remains wrapped. Place the lid of the box beneath the base for extra support. Using a sharp knife, score a lattice pattern (about ½cm deep) on the top of the cheese.

Gently push the rosemary, garlic and chilli into the top of the Camembert.

Place the Camembert, still in its box, on a baking tray, and bake for 15–20 minutes. The Camembert's rind should be unbroken and should not be browned. Allow the cheese to cool for a few minutes before serving it in the box, warm and gooey, and instruct your guests, 'Please reach for your cheese scoops!' These may be morsels of bread, cheese biscuits, sliced celery or pear, or spoons.

VARIATIONS

• Instead of Camembert, how about baking Cabécou, the soft goat's cheese from the Midi-Pyrénées? For a stunning example of British cheese, replace the Camembert with Tunworth, a cow's milk cheese from Hampshire.

• Before baking the cheese, spread the top of it with a spoonful of onion marmalade or your favourite chutney.

• For a truly decadent treat at Christmas, stud a whole Vacherin Mont d'Or (made from cow's milk) with small slivers of black truffle and then bake it, just as you would the Camembert.

Cheese Fondue

PREP 5 MINS / MELT 10 MINS, THEN REHEATED EVERY NOW AND AGAIN

Which came first, the fondue or the fondue set? Answer: the fondue. My point is, you do not need a fondue set to host a fondue night. Instead, the cheese can be melted in a large-ish casserole dish or heavy-based saucepan, and from time to time during the meal reheated on the hob. Fondue is French for 'melted', and it's just bread and cheese, but as they do it in the chalets on the ski slopes. On a cold, wintry night, guests gather around the warm melting pot, and the tone is set for togetherness. It's such a convivial dish, post coronavirus. I remember the wagers of my younger days – if you lost your bread in the fondue, you had to drink a glass of local wine in one go. Fondue also embodies the heart and soul of my region of Franche-Comté, where Comté cheese is a staple. Young Comté (aged about 12 months) is best for fondue, as the cheese becomes saltier with age. The finest sourdough bread is ideal; you want bread that's not crumbly – certainly not processed white sliced bread. Many other vegetables can be dipped, such as cooked potatoes, parsnips and raw celery, as well as diced smoked ham or sausage. Fondue is all about entertaining at home but without the cooking.

SERVES 4–6

600g Comté cheese (preferably 8–12 months old)
1 garlic clove
4 teaspoons cornflour
300ml dry white wine
3 tablespoons kirsch (optional but highly recommended)
ground black pepper

To serve
1 good-quality sourdough loaf

VARIATIONS

You can dip any raw vegetables cut into bite-sized pieces, such as mushrooms, cauliflower, carrot or pepper, or boiled new potatoes and gherkins.

TO PREPARE Grate the cheese and put it to one side. Peel the garlic, cut it in half and rub it around the inside of a medium-sized fondue pot (or casserole dish or heavy-based saucepan). Keep the garlic. Mix the cornflour with a little water, and put it to one side.

Place the pot on a high heat, pour in the wine and bring to a quick boil for 10 seconds, to remove some of the alcohol, and then reduce to a low heat. Stir the cornflour paste into the wine, which will instantly thicken.

Add about a third of the grated cheese to the hot pot and, over a low heat, stir slowly with a wooden spoon until it melts and is shiny. Then add another third and again, stir until it has completely melted, followed by the final third. It takes about a minute between each stage. If using kirsch – a touch of magic – add a dash now.

The fondue should have a smooth, thick-sauce texture. If it is too thin, add more cheese or stir in a little more cornflour, blended with water. If it is too thick or if it splits, stir in a little bit of water or wine from the bottle. The wine balances the dish with its acidity and helps with the emulsification of the fat in the cheese. Season with a little black pepper.

The fondue can be brought from the stove to the middle of the table on a board and then the feast can start. Serve with the bread, sliced into bite-sized pieces, and vegetables and any smoked meats you intend to serve, arranged in piles. Spear the bread on fondue forks, or simply table forks or skewers, and dip them into the runny fondue.

Croque Monsieur

PREP 5 MINS / COOK 20 MINS

The British adore their sandwich, the Americans love their burger. Croque Monsieur is the French cheese-bread snack, cherished comfort food that's been served for more than a century in cafés and bistros. Certainly, I've tried more than a few tired versions in the bars of my youth, but I am sure you will approve of this particular croque. The sandwich's béchamel sauce can also be used in so many other dishes, including chicken pies, fish pies and Italian pasta favourites – lasagne and cannelloni.

MAKES 2 GENEROUS SANDWICHES

For the béchamel sauce
50g extra-mature
    Cheddar cheese
250ml whole milk
25g unsalted butter
25g plain flour
1 tablespoon Dijon
    mustard
sea salt and black pepper

To build the croque monsieur
110g Comté cheese
    (I like 12-month-old
    Comté)
220g extra-mature
    Cheddar cheese
4 slices of sourdough
    or rye bread
6 slices of jambon de
    Paris ham
a handful of finely sliced
    chives (optional)

Preheat the grill to medium–high and the oven to 200°C/180°C fan/gas 6.

TO PREPARE Finely grate the Cheddar for the béchamel and the croque monsieur and the Comté.

First, make the béchamel sauce. Warm the milk in a small saucepan. In a medium-sized saucepan on a medium heat, melt the butter, add the flour and stir with a spatula to form a paste (known as a roux). Continue to cook for 2–3 minutes, stirring once or twice with the spatula.

Remove the pan from the heat, pour in the warm milk and stir with a whisk to blend well. Return the pan to the heat and increase the heat to high, stirring continuously with a whisk. Once the sauce has thickened, reduce the heat and let the sauce simmer gently for 1–2 minutes, until it's a silky-smooth béchamel.

Remove the pan from the heat and stir in the mustard and the grated Cheddar for the béchamel. Taste and adjust the seasoning accordingly. Put the pan to one side (or leave the sauce to cool and refrigerate until it's required).

Mix the Comté and remaining Cheddar together in a bowl. Under the grill, toast one side of the sourdough bread slices.

Build the two croque monsieurs on a baking tray lined with greaseproof paper. Spread about 1 dessertspoon of béchamel sauce on the untoasted side of each slice of toasted bread. Sprinkle half of the grated cheese mix on top of the four slices, and place three slices of ham on top of two of the slices of bread, which will become the base of the sandwiches, folding or cutting the slices of ham if necessary to fit. Sandwich together with the top slices of bread, toasted side up. When you have made both sandwiches, spoon the rest of the béchamel over the top.

Sprinkle with the remaining grated cheese and bake for 10–12 minutes, or until they are perfectly golden and grilled to your liking. Cut each sandwich in half, sprinkle with the chives, if using, and serve.

'When it comes to baking and
patisserie, the most essential equipment is
a good baking stone, a peel and a tart ring.
You'll be the best baker on the block.'

DESSERTS

Roasted Peaches

PREP 5 MINS / COOK 25 MINS

I have shared plenty of recipes with my son, Olivier, who is the creator of *Henri Le Worm*, a cookery app for children. Here is a recipe he shared with me … There is one crucial condition to this delightful, summery dessert – please try to use perfectly ripe peaches. Then let the heat create its own magic, as the fruit's flesh is roasted in a citrus syrup and becomes deliciously soft and highly scented. It takes about 30 minutes to make. Meanwhile, my yearly attempts at growing peaches have not produced fruit, but I shall not give up.

SERVES 4

4 large ripe peaches
1 tablespoon unsalted
  butter
2 tablespoons light
  brown sugar
juice of 3 oranges
juice of ¼ lemon
1 teaspoon vanilla bean
  paste or vanilla essence
  (or see Vanilla Bean
  Purée on page 297)
ice cream and/or crème
  fraîche

Preheat the oven to 190°C/170°C fan/gas 5.

Lay the peaches in an ovenproof dish. They should fit snugly – don't put them in a dish that's too large.

In a small saucepan on a medium heat, melt the butter and sugar together and cook for a couple of minutes to create a bubbling, golden caramel. Pour in the orange and lemon juices, stir and increase the heat to high. Let the mixture boil, reduce and thicken to become syrupy. Add the vanilla bean paste, stir and brush the syrup over the peaches.

Cover the peaches loosely with tinfoil or baking parchment and transfer them to the oven. Roast for 15–20 minutes, depending on their ripeness. Leave the peaches to cool slightly, and then serve them from the dish at the table, accompanied by ice cream or crème fraîche, or both.

VARIATIONS

• Instead of using whole peaches, you could also halve the peaches lengthways, remove the stones and roast in the dish skin-side down and cut-side up. This will reduce the roasting time.

• Replace the peaches with nectarines or apricots.

• To heighten the flavour of the syrup, add a dash of kirsch or peach liqueur.

• Before serving, scatter with crushed pistachio nuts, crushed biscuits or Crunchy Almonds (see page 260).

• Sometimes Olivier adds lavender to the caramel.

Stewed Apricots with Crunchy Almonds

PREP 5 MINS / COOK 15 MINS

This is such a lovely summer dessert – or breakfast – which I created during lockdown. With its vibrant colours, it looks hugely appetising. Then there's the tart-sweet taste of the ripe – they must be ripe – apricots. The gently stewed fruit is topped with sweet, crunchy baked almonds. They're like an alternative crumble mixture and can be a topping for many desserts, or scattered on ice cream. This dessert is best served warm, straight from the pan, and with cream, crème fraîche or ice cream. For breakfast, try it with a spoonful of yoghurt, and maybe miss out the kirsch.

SERVES 4

10 ripe apricots
40ml water
40g caster sugar
10g unsalted butter
juice of ½ lemon

For the crunchy almonds
80g flaked almonds
2 tablespoons water
  (or kirsch eau-de-vie)
30g icing sugar, plus a
  little extra for dusting

VARIATION

The same technique of stewing the fruits in caramel can be used for so many other fruits and berries (see the Apple and Blackberry Crumble on page 267).

Preheat the oven to 190°C/170°C fan/gas 5.

TO PREPARE Halve the apricots lengthways and remove the stones. Reserve.

Pour the water into a medium-sized deep-sided sauté pan or saucepan (about 25cm in diameter). Add the caster sugar and leave it for a few minutes to be absorbed. Bring to the boil on a medium–high heat and within a few minutes you will have a very pale, blond, thick syrup. Just before it becomes a caramel, add the butter and swirl the pan so that the syrup thickens and emulsifies.

Squeeze the lemon juice into the pan. (Tip: pour a little cold water into the squeezed lemon half and then squeeze again – this will extract the maximum amount of juice.)

Lastly, lay the apricot halves in the pan and stir gently. It'll be quite a tight fit for the apricots, but that's perfect. Cover the pan with a lid and reduce the heat to a very gentle simmer (too high and the apricots will fall apart). Cook like this for 10–15 minutes, depending on the ripeness of the apricots.

While the apricots are cooking, prepare the almonds. In a medium-sized bowl stir them with the water (or kirsch, if you are feeling rich). Next, sift the icing sugar over the almonds and stir again, so that they are sugar-coated. Spread the almonds evenly on a baking tray and bake in the preheated oven for 9–10 minutes, until golden.

Remove the tray from the oven and leave them to cool for a few minutes. You will have crusty clusters of golden, baked almonds.

Serve the stewed apricots at the table straight from the pan, or transfer them to a shallow serving dish. Just before serving, scatter the almonds over the warm apricots.

Strawberry and Mascarpone Tart

PREP 10 MINS / CHILL 1 HOUR (OPTIONAL)

A crowd-pleaser extraordinaire, and so easy to make. Light, crisp and with a blend of strawberries, mascarpone creaminess and raspberry jam, this is an excellent tart for a summer's day. It is a sweet conclusion to a barbecue, or a treat to pack in a picnic. Of course, you can make your own pastry. However, you may prefer a shop-bought, prebaked pastry case. In which case, if you have time, a little tip: place the pastry case in an oven preheated to 180°C/160°C fan/gas 4 until it has achieved a golden biscuit colour. By baking it again, you give back life to the pastry, adding colour, texture and, ultimately, flavour. Small pastry tartlet cases can also be used.

SERVES 6–8

1 shortcrust pastry case, precooked, about 20cm diameter (shop-bought or see page 296)
icing sugar, for dusting

For the filling
400g strawberries
500g mascarpone
50ml double cream
1 teaspoon vanilla bean paste or vanilla essence (or see Vanilla Bean Purée on page 297)
½ lemon
200g raspberry jam, preferably seedless

TO PREPARE Wash and hull the strawberries.

In a large bowl, mix the mascarpone, double cream and vanilla bean paste and add the zest of the lemon half. Put aside.

Spread the raspberry jam onto the base of the pastry case. Spoon half the mascarpone mixture over the top of the jam and spread it over the tart – don't worry if it mixes with the jam. Now spread the rest of the mascarpone mixture on top. (Use a piping bag to pipe the mascarpone onto the jam, if you prefer.)

Next, the decoration of this summer tart. How should you cut the strawberries for the top? It's your choice – you can try slices, halves or quarters. Or if you have lots of small strawberries, leave them whole and stand them upright on top of the tart.

Once you have decorated the top of the tart with the strawberries, and if you have time, transfer the tart to the fridge for up to 1 hour. Chilling the filling means neat slicing. Remove from the fridge, dust with icing sugar and serve.

Blanc Manger with Raspberry Coulis

PREP 35 MINS / COOK 5 MINS / CHILL 4 HOURS

You may shudder and want to turn this page as you recall the pink and watery blancmange from school days. I advise you to stay here, with me. Blancmange wasn't served at my school (I was eating delicious *petits pots au chocolat*), but for my sins, many years ago I wrote a book, *Blanc Mange*. I thought it was one of the favourite desserts of the British. Little did I know. Anyway, this dessert is similarly named but entirely different in taste. It is light, unusual and refreshing, and the almond syrup imparts so much character. The colourful raspberry compote, meanwhile, can also be made in advance. A beautiful little dish, it is always popular and will restore your faith in blancmange.

SERVES 4

4 gelatine leaves
300ml whole milk
60ml almond syrup/
   cordial
200ml double cream

For the raspberry coulis
250g raspberries
15g caster sugar

Soak the gelatine leaves in a bowl of cold water for about 5 minutes.

Meanwhile, in a medium saucepan on a medium heat, warm the milk and almond syrup. When it starts to simmer, remove the pan from the heat.

Squeeze the water from the gelatine leaves, and add them to the pan. Stir well with a whisk to dissolve the gelatine, and pour the mixture into a bowl and leave it for about 20 minutes – you want it to cool to just above room temperature but not set, about 30°C (90°F) if using a thermometer. (The bowl can be placed in another bowl of iced water to speed up the cooling process.)

In a separate bowl, whip the cream to medium peaks. Use a hand whisk to fold and stir the whipped cream into the cooled milk-almond mixture.

Divide the mixture equally into four pudding moulds (or ramekins), ensuring it almost fills them. Refrigerate for at least 4 hours, until fully set.

To remove each one from its mould:

1. Place the mould in warm water for a few seconds, depending on the thickness of the mould.

2. Put a dessert plate on the top of the pudding mould, and now turn the two over together so that it drops out of the mould onto the plate.

3. The Blanc Manger might need to be helped along with a little shake.

For the raspberry coulis, which can be made in advance, take half the raspberries and purée with the caster sugar in a blender. Pass through a fine sieve to remove the seeds. Mix the sieved coulis with the remaining whole raspberries and reserve in the fridge until ready to serve with the Blanc Manger.

Apple and Blackberry Crumble

PREP 15 MINS / COOK 30 MINS

The British crumble is a classic home comfort, often served after the Sunday roast. It has a crunchy top that's also gooey and stodgy where it meets the fruit beneath. I have watched people eat crumble and then leave the table, ballooned and unwell. What is the point in creating a dessert that's going to kill you? The whole idea of crumble is that sensation of crunch, sweetness and the biscuity flavour. The first time I made this light-crumble version it went down well. Years later, and I am still making it. Serve the crumble with clotted cream, crème fraîche or vanilla custard or ice cream. For the apple varieties in this dish, I like to use Cox, Blenheim Orange or Bramley. The crumble topping and apple compote can be prepared a day in advance and kept separately in sealed containers in the fridge.

SERVES 6–8

Preheat the oven to 200°C/180°C fan/gas 6.

For the crumble topping
120g plain flour
120g Demerara sugar
60g unsalted butter, at room temperature and cut into 2cm pieces

TO PREPARE Peel, core and quarter the apples, then cut each quarter in half to create eight roughly square pieces from each apple. Put in a large saucepan with the water and cover with a lid.

In a large bowl, mix the flour and sugar. Add the butter pieces, and mix them in with the tips of your fingers to achieve a sandy texture. This will take 4–5 minutes. Next, mix with your hands, creating nuggets of raw crumble. Scatter this crumble topping directly onto a baking tray. Bake for 15 minutes until rich and golden. Remove the tray and scrape the mixture with a spatula to break some of the larger pieces. Leave the crumble to cool on the tray.

For the apple compote
6 medium/large apples
2 tablespoons water
1 teaspoon vanilla bean paste or vanilla essence (or see Vanilla Bean Purée on page 297) (optional)

Now, the apples. Place the apples and water in the saucepan on a high heat, add the vanilla bean paste, bring to the boil, then reduce to a simmer. Simmer for 8–10 minutes, until the apples start to break down.

For the blackberries (picked from the hedges, if you can)
20g caster sugar
15g unsalted butter, cold
230g blackberries

Next, the blackberries. In a frying pan on a medium heat, melt the caster sugar into a syrup and add the butter. Swirl the pan to melt the butter, then add the blackberries. Stir and cook for 1 minute. Remove from the heat and reserve.

Serve in a large serving dish or in individual bowls. Spoon in the blackberries, cover with apple compote and then top with the gorgeous crumble.

Serve with clotted cream, crème fraîche, custard or ice cream.

Tarte Boulangère

PREP 15 MINS / COOK 50 MINS

Or baker's tart. So called because for centuries it has been prepared by nimble, floury fingers in every bakery in France. A pillar of French tradition, this dessert is also very simple, unrefined and rustic – bakers did not aspire to be the finest pâtissiers. With the availability of good-quality puff pastry, it is even easier to make these days. It's delicious and a joy to cook at home, using British-grown apples. The lid-less tart can be prepared in advance and served at room temperature, or gently reheated in the oven and served warm. Apricots, plums, figs and most fruits make a delicious substitute for apples.

SERVES 4–6

plain flour, for dusting
300g all-butter puff pastry
  (block or ready-rolled)
5–6 Royal Gala, Cox or
  Braeburn apples (total
  weight 700–800g)
50g unsalted butter
5 dessertspoons (about
  85g) Demerara sugar
1 teaspoon ground
  cinnamon
juice of ½ lemon
1 tablespoon Calvados
  (or water, if you must)

To finish
a handful of flaked
  almonds (optional)
icing sugar, for dusting

VARIATION

Roast flaked almonds or crushed hazelnuts in the oven and sprinkle over when you serve.

Preheat the oven to 200°C/180°C fan/gas 6.

Pastry first. On a floured board, roll out a disc of pastry that's about 4mm thick. If using ready-rolled, simply unroll your pastry. Place a cake tin of about 18cm diameter on the pastry and cut around it, to create a disc of puff pastry. Run a sharp knife around the pastry, about 1cm from the edge, and about 1mm deep. This concentric circle will enable the pastry to rise perfectly around the apples. Line a baking tray, and place the disc onto it. Reserve in the fridge.

Peel and core the apples. Halve each apple lengthways, and cut each half into three equal-sized segments lengthways.

Melt the butter and mix it on a separate baking tray with the Demerara sugar, cinnamon, lemon juice and the Calvados (or water). Roll the apple segments in the sugary mixture, so that they are well coated.

Roast for 10 minutes. Turn over the apple pieces, baste them, and return them to the oven for a further 10 minutes. Remove the tray from the oven, and reduce the oven temperature to 190°C/170°C fan/gas 5. Baste the apples once more, and leave them to cool.

Arrange the apple segments on top of the pastry in a circle – leaving the space of about 1cm from the edge of the disc – to form a dome of apple pieces. Brush them with the remaining syrup from the baking tray.

Bake in the oven (at the reduced temperature of 190°C) for 25–30 minutes.

Enjoy Tarte Boulangère warm or at room temperature. Sprinkle with flaked almonds, if using, dust with a little icing sugar and serve with a jug of cream, a bowl of whipped cream or with ice cream or crème fraîche.

My love for
APPLES

Ah, symbol of love, fertility and good fortune, the apple is also the embodiment of good health – 'An apple a day keeps the doctor away'. And this fruit starred in a great story about Adam and Eve. As a crumble it has helped to sustain Britain through war and peace. As tarte Tatin it is an emblem of French cuisine, while ownership of the apple pie is claimed, whether rightly or wrongly, by the Americans.

When I was growing up in the village of Saône in Franche-Comté, we had an apple tree that gave us plenty of Reinette, a tasty little variety that's adored by the French, and much of the harvest went into my mother's unbeatable apple tart. Life moves on. Decades later, at Le Manoir, we planted an orchard of 2,500 trees, which includes 151 varieties of apple. Some of the coxes are used to make Apple Tart Maman Blanc, following my mother's recipe. At a time when Britain is losing its orchards, this one is a testament to my love of the apple. I am also extremely proud to be an ambassador for British Apples & Pears, an organisation of growers who supply the highest quality homegrown produce.

Do taste apples before cooking with them, though there are only about 8,000 varieties to sample. If you take a number of apples from a tree, store them and taste one every few days, you will notice how the flavour improves. Some experts say that Christmas is the best time to eat an apple. Queen Victoria, like you and I, enjoyed baked apples. I brush them with melted butter, roll them in caster sugar and bake them at 170°C/150°C fan/gas 3½ for about 40 minutes. Meanwhile, I make a dark caramel – a splash of apple juice added at the end (and even a dash of Calvados or cider). The hot caramel is poured over the warm baked apple. A scoop of vanilla ice cream is compulsory.

Sticky Toffee Pudding

PREP 10 MINS / COOK 30 MINS

Along with crumble, this has to be one of my favourite desserts. Sticky toffee pudding is a great British triumph, which deserves international acclaim. With a scoop of vanilla ice cream, or with custard or double cream, it is almost beyond hugely satisfying. I think it's a genius dish and, intrigued, I have been researching its history. The original recipe, I discover, was taken and developed in the 1970s by Francis Coulson at Sharrow Bay, a remarkable country house hotel in the Lake District. Once upon a time it was the place to stay. Well, I am honoured to have known Francis and his partner, Brian Sack. He was a culinary legend, bon viveur and gentleman. I revere both the dessert and the chef and, now that I am aware of the association, I love this pudding twice as much.

SERVES 4

For the pudding
130g pitted dates
225ml water
1 level teaspoon
  bicarbonate of soda
1 tablespoon Vanilla Bean
  Purée (see page 297) or
  use 1 teaspoon vanilla
  bean paste or vanilla
  essence
40g unsalted butter
130g dark muscovado
  sugar
2 medium eggs
  (preferably organic
  or free-range)
130g plain flour

For the sauce
65g unsalted butter
90g Demerara sugar
90ml double cream

Preheat the oven to 170°C/150°C fan/gas 3½.

We'll make the pudding first, and then the sauce …

Place the dates, water, bicarbonate of soda and vanilla purée in a saucepan, bring to the boil and simmer for 5 minutes until the dates have softened. Mash with a fork and leave to cool slightly.

Meanwhile, in a bowl cream together the butter and sugar until light in colour. Add the eggs and mix well.

Add the date mixture to the butter, sugar and eggs, sift in the flour and fold together until the flour is completely mixed in.

Pour into a deep baking tray lined with greaseproof paper and bake for 20–25 minutes. To check it is cooked, insert a small knife into the middle of the pudding – if it comes out clean, you are there! Leave to cool for 10 minutes, and reserve or portion when cooled.

Meanwhile, make the caramel sauce. In a saucepan, add the butter and sugar and cook over a medium heat until it's a dark golden caramel. Remove from the heat, add the cream and stir until it has cooled. Reserve.

Finally, we can savour this fantastic dessert. I feel you may not need my advice for serving, but here goes anyway … Place a portion of the pudding in the middle of a bowl, pour over some of the warm sticky toffee sauce and serve with a scoop of vanilla ice cream, custard or double cream.

Chocolates and Truffles

PREP 5 MINS / COOK 10 MINS / SET 1 HOUR

Making chocolates brings out the child in all of us, and perhaps you will find a young, curious helper (or two) and then put on your aprons and set aside a little time to have fun.

**MAKES 40–50
CHOCOLATES
OR TRUFFLES**

300g dark chocolate,
   about 70% cocoa solids
300ml whipping cream
   (or double cream)
35g honey
60g unsalted butter,
   diced small

For the coatings
125g cocoa powder,
   finely chopped pistachio
   nuts, toasted chopped
   almonds, desiccated
   coconut or crushed
   dried raspberries

In a microwave or a bowl over a saucepan of simmering water, melt the 70% chocolate (to around 40°C/105°F, if using a thermometer).

Separately, in a small saucepan, bring the cream and honey to the boil. Remove the pan from the heat and, little by little, whisk the boiled cream-honey into the melted chocolate. The mix may look like it is splitting, but persevere and keep adding the cream mix, little by little, and you will end up with a shiny, silky-smooth mix. Continue to stir with a spatula until the mixture has cooled to 35–40°C (95–105°F). Test by touching it to your bottom lip – it will be slightly warm to the touch.

With the spatula, stir in the butter. This is the stage at which to add any flavours you would like (see Variations, below). Or you can keep it plain.

For chocolates: if you would like to make bite-sized squares, pour the mixture into a shallow lined tray or container (leave a little overhang with the lining, so it's easy to remove from the tray). Allow the mixture to set before turning it out and cutting it in squares (or desired shapes).

For truffles: pour the mixture into a deep bowl and leave it to set. Use a melon baller to scoop out truffles and place them on a lined tray.

To coat the chocolates, give them a dusting of cocoa powder, turn them over and dust again. For the truffles, roll them in the cocoa powder. Alternatively, roll the chocolates in any of the coatings listed on the left.

VARIATIONS

• Experiment with different chocolates: replace the 70% dark chocolate with 500g of 40% milk chocolate or 590g white chocolate. After incorporating the butter, flavour the chocolate with your choice of alcohol: rum, whisky, brandy or cassis.

• Fruit purée: instead of the cream, use a raspberry purée.

• Infusion: before bringing the cream to the boil with the honey, infuse it by adding a flavour. Try Earl Grey tea, fresh mint or cinnamon, then strain the cream before bringing it to the boil with the honey. For instance, add 40g Earl Grey tea and leave for 1 minute before straining through a sieve. Double check you still have 300ml for the recipe and top up if necessary, then add the honey and bring to the boil, ready to mix into the melted chocolate.

Pear Almondine

PREP 10 MINS / COOK 25 MINS

It's rare to find a dessert that is both simple and extraordinarily delicious. Pear Almondine is one of my favourites. You can find some excellent preserved Williams pears in jars or tins, ideal for this recipe. Most cooks use a tart ring with a base. The problem is it takes twice as long to cook the pastry and often the pastry is uncooked. So may I recommend three tools that will help your baking. 1. A tart ring with no base to it; 2. A baker's peel, to slide the tart ring into the oven; 3. A baking stone or pizza stone, which will radiate the heat. The dough sits directly on greaseproof paper on the hot baking stone. You can use an upturned baking tray instead of a stone, but if you love baking, the peel and stone will make it so much easier.

SERVES 6

4–6 pear halves, tinned or jarred
100g unsalted butter, at room temperature, plus extra for brushing the tin
100g caster sugar
100g ground almonds
1 teaspoon cornflour
1 teaspoon vanilla bean paste or vanilla essence (or see Vanilla Bean Purée on page 297) (optional)
1 medium egg (preferably organic or free-range)
a handful of flaked almonds (for extra flavour, first toast them in a dry pan)
icing sugar, for dusting

Preheat the oven to 200°C/180°C fan/gas 6.

Butter (or oil) a tart ring, about 18cm x 2cm. Cut a long strip of greaseproof paper to line the inside of the buttered tart ring. Place the buttered and lined tart ring onto a flat baking sheet, upturned baking tray or baker's peel lined with greaseproof paper. Place a separate tray or baking stone on the middle shelf of the preheated oven, ready to slide the pear tart onto to ensure the heat begins to cook directly into the base of the tart.

Drain the pears and slice them in half again if they are large. In a large bowl, mix the softened butter and sugar. Then add the ground almonds, cornflour, vanilla bean paste and egg, and mix well. Spoon the mixture into the tart ring, spreading it evenly.

Arrange the pear halves evenly around the outside of the tart, resting them on top of the almond sponge mixture, and with the tip of each half meeting in the middle. According to the size of the pears, you may require the base of half a pear to fill a space in the centre. Scatter with almonds.

Slide the pear tart onto the preheated tray or baking stone and bake for 20–25 minutes, or until golden.

Leave the cake to cool for a few minutes before removing it from the ring. Before serving, dust with icing sugar.

VARIATION

In a saucepan, reduce the syrup from the jar, let it cool and add a dash of Poire William, the pear liqueur. After baking, puncture the pears with a fork and pour over the syrup. It adds colour and flavour.

Cut and Come Again Cake

PREP 10 MINS / COOK 1 HOUR

Once upon a time there was a Cornish woman who loved to cook. Lilian Gladys Johnson was her name. She baked lots of cakes, and one of her favourites was a fruitcake. She called it her 'cut and come again cake', and it sat on a table, but not for long because her family helped themselves, cutting a slice … and coming again, for another slice, or a pinch of moist crumbs.

Well, with all that baking she was lucky to have a helper, her little grandson Adam. It was there, in the kitchen with his grandmother – and with his mother – that young Adam discovered a real enthusiasm for cooking. He grew up to become a chef. The story is sweeter still because I am proud to call Adam Johnson my protégé. I am also honoured to share that recipe for his grandmother's cut and come again cake.

Adam, known as Adaaaam, is a constant companion. Together we create magnificent moments for others, be it in Jardin Blanc at Chelsea Flower Show, cooking in kitchens across the world or making our next television series. Or indeed, writing this beautiful book. I tease Adam. For example on camera, I ask him to say, '*Vive la France,*' or sing 'La Marseillaise' – I got the late Queen Mother to sing it, why not Adam? – but to no avail. Adam is a true traditionalist and close to his terroir.

I have a wish. It is to go to Cornwall and go fishing together for mackerel. We'll be in our little boat on the glittering, turquoise seas, with mackerel jumping around us. Of course, I will be catching the big ones; Adam, the little ones. On a beach, we'll barbecue the fish and feed Adam's family, giving the best to his beloved grandfather, Sidney Johnson MBE. The day will be filled with laughter.

MAKES 8 SLICES

225g self-raising flour
¼ teaspoon salt
1 teaspoon mixed spice
110g butter or margarine, cold and diced
110g caster sugar
250g dried fruits
1 medium egg (preferably organic or free-range)
1 teaspoon grated or zested orange or lemon zest
50ml water
50ml whole milk (or another 50ml water)

Preheat the oven to 160°C/140°C fan/gas 3.

Sift together the flour, salt and mixed spice.

Rub the butter into the flour mixture until you have a breadcrumb texture. Stir in the sugar and dried fruits.

Now, make a well in the middle. With a fork, whisk together the egg, zest, water and milk. Mix this into the flour mixture.

Pour the mixture into a suitably sized lined cake tin (whatever you have). Bake for 30 minutes, and then reduce the oven temperature to 150°C/130°C fan/gas 2 and continue to bake for a further 30 minutes.

Allow the cake to cool for a few minutes before removing from the tin and then transferring it to a wire rack to cool to room temperature.

Leave the cake on a board, with a knife beside it, and invite family and your many friends to cut and come again … and again.

Coconut Panna Cotta, Mango and Passion Fruit

PREP 15 MINS / COOK 15 MINS / SET 2–3 HOURS

SERVES 4

For the coconut panna cotta
2½ gelatine leaves
400ml coconut milk
juice of ½ lime
2 tablespoons Malibu
   liqueur
50g palm or caster sugar
1 teaspoon Vanilla Bean
   Purée (see page 297)
   or ½ teaspoon good
   vanilla essence
5–6 kaffir lime leaves

For the fruit layer
½ small mango
a few mint or lemon
   verbena sprigs
2 passion fruit
a few turns of ground
   black pepper or a pinch
   of cayenne pepper

*For the mango foam
(optional but adds a new
dimension – perhaps for
a special occasion)*
½ small mango
juice of ½ lime
2 medium egg whites
   (preferably organic
   or free-range)
40g caster sugar

To finish (optional)
passion fruit or
   pomegranate seeds,
   mango chunks,
   shredded mint or
   lemon balm leaves

Natalia and I were on holiday in the Maldives, and within stretching distance of the freshest ingredients – coconut, pineapple, mango, passion fruit. That is when I borrowed the hotel's kitchen and created this dish. You can keep it simple, by making just the panna cotta topped by the colourful exotic fruits and herbs. Or, for a special occasion, follow the whole recipe. For a vegan version, replace the gelatine with agar agar, using 1g of agar to 100ml of liquid, although the agar jelly will set hard.

Soak the gelatine leaves in a bowl of cold water for at least 5 minutes, to soften them. In a medium saucepan on a high heat, bring to a simmer the coconut milk, lime juice, Malibu, sugar, vanilla purée and kaffir lime leaves.

Stir in the softened gelatine leaves, take off the heat and stir every now and again for 5 minutes. Strain through a fine sieve. Pour the panna cotta mixture into four glasses or ramekin moulds and leave to set in the fridge for at least 2–3 hours.

To make the fruit layer, peel the mango and dice half of it (the other mango half will be used for the foam). Finely chop the mint or verbena leaves. In a bowl mix the mango, passion fruit pulp and seeds (keep some passion fruit seeds aside) and mint. To lift the flavours, add a few turns of black pepper or a tiny pinch of cayenne pepper.

Top the set panna cotta with the fruit mix. Scatter with the reserved passion fruit seeds. It's now ready to serve, or refrigerate if you intend to make the mango foam.

To make the mango foam, purée the remaining mango half with a stick blender or a small grinder and stir in the lime juice. Reserve in a bowl.

Whisk the egg whites on a high speed and, when they start to foam, incorporate the caster sugar little by little. Whisk to very stiff peaks.

Take a third of the whisked egg whites and briskly whisk them with the purée. Next, fold in the remaining two-thirds of the stiffened egg whites.

Top each panna cotta with the foam. Scatter with some of the passion fruit or pomegranate seeds, mango and the mint or lemon balm, if using.

Flourless Chocolate Mousse Cake

PREP 20 MINS / COOK 30 MINS / SET 3 HOURS

A chocolate mousse cake with no flour required. It's such a fabulous dessert – extremely popular with 'students' at the Raymond Blanc Cookery School and a must-do recipe for children. The sponge can be made in advance and then kept in the freezer for a day or two. I have used a cake tin with a diameter of 15cm, but simply adapt to fit your favourite tin size.

SERVES 8–10

*For the flourless
chocolate sponge*
butter, for greasing the tin
4 medium eggs
  (preferably organic
  or free-range)
125g caster sugar
35g cocoa powder

For the chocolate mousse
160g dark chocolate
  (70% cocoa solids)
25g cocoa powder
1 medium egg yolk
  (preferably organic or
  free-range)
3 tablespoons hot water
6 medium egg whites
  (preferably organic or
  free-range)
25g caster sugar

To serve (optional)
cocoa powder, for dusting
grated dark chocolate
a handful of pistachio
  nuts or almonds,
  chopped and toasted
  in a dry pan

Preheat the oven to 170°C/150°C fan/gas 3½.

Begin by making the chocolate sponge in a cake tin (preferably a springform one, 15cm diameter). Cut a circle of greaseproof paper to cover the tin's base, and lightly butter the paper on both sides.

Separate the eggs – yolks in one bowl, whites in another. In a food mixer on full power, whisk the egg whites to firm peaks, adding the sugar little by little. Take a third of the whisked egg whites and whisk them into the egg yolks. Once incorporated, gently fold in the remaining whisked whites. Now sift and fold in the cocoa powder.

Pour the mixture into the prepared cake tin and spread it evenly with a spatula or palette knife. Bake for 18–20 minutes, or until a skewer inserted into the middle comes out clean. Allow the sponge to cool before removing it from the tin. Leave it to cool on a wire rack.

Clean the cake tin. Carefully remove the paper from the base of the sponge. Now put the cooled sponge back in the ring, ready to have the chocolate mousse mixture poured over it.

Chop the chocolate into bite-sized pieces and melt them in a large heatproof bowl in a saucepan of gently simmering water. The melted chocolate should be hot to the touch to ensure it is well incorporated in the next stage. Sift the cocoa powder into a separate bowl and whisk it with the egg yolk and hot water. Pour this onto the melted chocolate but do not mix.

Next, whisk the egg whites and sugar to medium peaks. Briskly whisk about a third of the whisked egg whites into the melted chocolate, and then fold in the remaining egg whites.

Pour the mousse mixture onto the chocolate sponge in the ring. Transfer it to the fridge to set for at least 3 hours.

To remove the flourless chocolate mousse cake, heat a palette knife in a bowl of hot water, wipe it with a clean tea towel, and then slide it around the inside of the tin. Before serving, decorate with a dusting of cocoa, a sprinkling of grated chocolate and chopped toasted pistachios or almonds, if using.

Jasmine Milk Pots

PREP 15 MINS / COOK 45 MINS / COOL 30 MINS

Often, I am asked for a recipe for a simple dessert with few ingredients. This one comes to mind. Creamy, rich and silky, the sweetness of the milk pot is balanced by the lemon in the syrup. For best results, use good-quality jasmine tea leaves in the infusion. For chocolate pots, replace the jasmine with 100g dark chocolate (70% cocoa solids).

SERVES 4

For the milk pots
500ml whole milk
70g caster sugar
a small handful (about 10g) of jasmine tea, or a bunch of lemon verbena
6 medium egg yolks (preferably organic or free-range)

For the lemon syrup
2 lemons
30g caster sugar
2 tablespoons water

Preheat the oven to 180°C/160°C fan/gas 4.

Let's begin by making the milk pots, and then the syrup.

In a large saucepan, and over a high heat, bring the milk and sugar to a simmer. Add the jasmine tea (or lemon verbena), remove the pan from the heat and leave to infuse until the mixture cools to room temperature.

Strain the mixture into a large bowl and whisk in the egg yolks. Divide this mixture into four large ramekins or ovenproof pots.

Prepare a bain-marie: a deep baking tray with enough hot water to come about two-thirds of the way up the sides of the ramekins. Cover the ramekins with a sheet of foil and bake for 15 minutes.

Reduce the oven temperature to 160°C/140°C fan/gas 3, remove the foil and bake for a further 20 minutes.

Remove the ramekins from the tin and leave them to cool. Once cooled, cover with non-pvc clingfilm and refrigerate until required.

Now for the lemon syrup …

Finely grate the zest of the two lemons and squeeze the juice from one. Slice the other lemon into segments, and then cut the segments into small pieces and keep them to one side.

Place the zest and juice in a small saucepan and add the sugar and water. Bring to the boil and continue to cook for a minute or so until it is syrupy. Remove the pan from the heat and stir in the small pieces of lemon.

When the syrup has cooled, spoon it over the milk pots and serve.

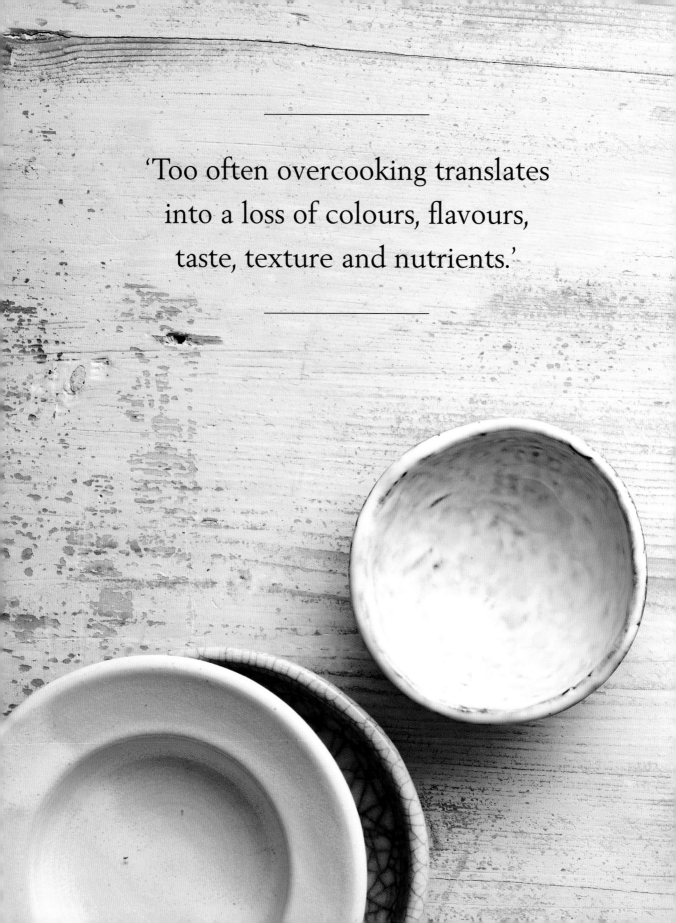

'Too often overcooking translates
into a loss of colours, flavours,
taste, texture and nutrients.'

RB'S BASIC RECIPES

―――――――――

'Today we have the best
opportunity to reconnect
with our local values,
agriculture and our own
heritage close to home.'

―――――――――

Red Wine Sauce

PREP 5 MINS / COOK 25 MINS

Full of flavour, red wine sauce is also rich and lavish, and what my British friends might describe as 'posh gravy'. It adds a touch of grandeur to pan-fried or grilled meats, such as steak, and goes well with the robust fish, brill and turbot. As for red wine sauce with the Sunday roast – well, you could say, it's the icing on the cake. There are some points to note. The wine, which is reduced to remove most of the alcohol and soften the tannins, should be inexpensive and powerful (by which I mean strong). Try a hearty red from sunny Périgord, such as Côtes de Bergerac, or Côtes du Rhône. Field mushrooms are the best type for this sauce. They add intense flavour and depth of colour. White onion is the sweetest (and perhaps the cheapest) variety to use. This sauce can be prepared in advance and with one certainty – as you cook it, your kitchen will be filled with aromas to make your mouth water.

SERVES 4

1 white onion
4 field mushrooms
30g unsalted butter
2 thyme sprigs
6 whole black
  peppercorns
300ml red wine
400ml good-quality
  shop-bought
  chicken stock
1 small tarragon sprig
1 tablespoon cornflour
  (or arrowroot)
4 tablespoons cold water

VARIATION

The wine can be reduced in a separate pan, if you wish, and then added to the onions and mushrooms once they are at their golden stage. This will slightly speed up the cooking time, and the finished sauce will be clearer.

TO PREPARE This sauce is really a lesson in the benefits of reduction: less, as you shall taste, is certainly more. Start at the chopping board … Finely dice the onion and coarsely chop the field mushrooms. Put these to one side.

Now you can begin to cook … In a medium-sized saucepan and on a medium heat, melt the butter and, when it foams, add the onion and sweat for 1–2 minutes. Stir, add the mushrooms, thyme and peppercorns and increase the heat to medium–high. Cook for a further 3–4 minutes, or until the onion and mushrooms are golden, and stir occasionally to prevent sticking or burning.

Pour the wine into the saucepan, increase the heat and bring to a full boil. Continue to boil until the wine has reduced in volume by half. This will take about 5 minutes. Pour in the chicken stock and bring the sauce back to the boil on a high heat. Let it reduce by about a third. Skim away any impurities from the surface. Next, add the tarragon and cook for a further minute or two. Taste and correct the seasoning – you may feel a pinch or two of sugar is required, but no salt should be necessary.

Now, the last stage – thickening the sauce. In a bowl, mix the cornflour (or arrowroot) with the cold water. Add a ladleful of the hot sauce, stir and then whisk this mixture into the red wine sauce (thus preventing lumps). Bring back to the boil and simmer for 1 minute to thicken the sauce.

Strain this gorgeous sauce and serve immediately. As for the mushrooms? Enjoy them later on a slice of buttered toast. Alternatively, leave the sauce to cool, and then store it in the fridge or in the freezer.

Oven-dried Tomatoes and Olives

PREP 5 MINS / COOK 2 HOURS

The drying of foods beneath the sun is the oldest form of food preservation. Consider the grape that becomes the raisin or sultana. Think of the plum that turns into the prune. The sun not only preserves but also intensifies flavour and sweetness. The fresh fig, for instance, is so very different once dried. Ancient man depended on the sun to be the cook, but we can recreate the process in an oven. In the slowest heat behind the closed door of your oven, the tomatoes and olives are dried (or, to be specific, semi-dried) as if they were being gently baked by the Mediterranean sun (see photo on pages 310–11). This is a Provençal-style garnish to serve with grilled and pan-fried fish and meat, and ideal for those sunny days beside the barbecue. If you prefer to use plum tomatoes rather than cherry, these should be quartered and the seeds removed. Many other vegetables can be dried, and fruits such as apples, pears, raspberries, strawberries and plums.

**MAKES ENOUGH
FOR 4–6 SERVINGS**

2 dozen cherry tomatoes
5 handfuls of black olives,
    pitted
a few thyme sprigs
    (optional)
pinch of sea salt flakes

Preheat the oven to 80°C/60°C fan/gas ¼.

TO PREPARE Slice the tomatoes in half lengthways.

Place the tomatoes, olives and thyme sprigs, if using, on a baking tray and spread them out evenly. Sprinkle over the salt.

Bake for 2 hours.

The tomatoes and olives are semi-dried so can be stored for up to a week in a sealed airtight container in the fridge.

Boiled Rice

PREP 5 MINS / COOK 30 MINS / SOAK 30 MINS

This recipe has also been given to me by Shailesh Kumar Jha and will go very well with his Vegetable Kadai (see page 212). 'Many different types of rice are eaten every day in India,' Shailesh tells me, 'but basmati is perhaps the best known one, at least in North India. The previous year's rice is older and considered better than the new rice.' He adds, 'It is difficult to generalise cooking different varieties of rice. The method below is best for basmati or other long-grain rice. Brown rice needs more water and longer cooking times.'

SHAILESH'S KEY POINTS TO KNOW BEFORE COOKING RICE

• For basmati rice, use approximately ⅓ cup (or 60–70g) rice per person. My mum used to say, 'One good fistful per person,' and it works for me.

• The amount of water depends on which method of cooking you use. Less water is needed if you have soaked the rice in advance.

• Indians do not run cold water on cooked rice, as the rice is almost always served immediately, fresh and hot. However, this is a good thing to do if you are going to use the rice for a stir-fry, which requires cold rice. Running cold water will stop it from cooking further and getting lumpy.

SERVES 4

250g basmati rice
500ml recently boiled water
1 teaspoon salt
1 tablespoon vegetable oil

TO PREPARE Wash the rice gently in cold water, until the water runs clean. This is to remove dust and excess starch, so the end result is not sticky. Soaking it for 30 minutes or so makes it longer and fluffier. Before cooking, strain the rice in a colander or sieve to drain off all the water.

First, measure the water – twice the amount by volume, which is 2 cups of water for 1 cup of rice. Bring the measured water to the boil in a flat-bottomed pan (it will need a tight-fitting lid – but not yet). Add the salt and vegetable oil. Bring the water to boil.

Add the drained rice and bring to the boil again. After about 20 seconds of brisk boiling and bubbling, place the lid on the pan, and reduce the heat to minimum.

Cook for 10–15 minutes on a low heat, until all the water is absorbed. Do not keep lifting the lid – keep peeking to nil or a minimum. I often cook rice in a glass-lidded pan, so there is no temptation to lift the lid.

At the end of cooking, when the water is nearly gone or gone, open the lid gently and pick up a couple of rice grains. To check if it is ready, squeeze the grains between your finger and thumb – no grit should be felt.

Allow the rice to rest or stand, still covered, for 5–10 minutes before serving. This ensures that all the rice is evenly cooked. Lightly fluff up the rice with a fork, and serve hot with a dhal or a curry of meat, chicken, fish or vegetables.

Tartare Sauce

PREP 3 MINS

The perfect sauce to serve with fishcakes or fish in batter, such as the Smoked Haddock Beignets (see page 45). It's also extremely easy to make mayonnaise (see recipe on page 111) or vegan mayonnaise using the water from a tin of chickpeas (see page 63).

MAKES 220G

60g gherkins
25g capers
125g mayonnaise,
  Greek yoghurt or skyr
2 teaspoons Dijon
  mustard or horseradish
  sauce (optional)
pinch of cayenne pepper

TO PREPARE Finely chop the gherkins and capers.

Mix the gherkins and capers with the mayonnaise (or yoghurt) and add the Dijon mustard, or horseradish sauce, if using. Add a pinch of cayenne pepper. Taste and add a little more of this or that, accordingly.

Sauce Gribiche

PREP 5 MINS / COOK 10 MINS

A creamy, piquant alternative to Tartare, this condiment is also quick to make and delicious with fish – pan-fried, shallow-fried, deep-fried, barbecued or grilled.

MAKES ABOUT 150G

2 medium eggs
  (preferably organic
  or free-range)
½ small shallot
1–2 small cornichons
2 teaspoons capers
2–3 flat-leaf parsley sprigs
1 teaspoon Dijon
  mustard
3 tablespoons
  mayonnaise
pinch of sea salt flakes
small pinch of cayenne
  pepper

TO PREPARE Hard-boil the eggs for 10–12 minutes, refresh in cold water, peel them and finely chop (or grate) the whites of both eggs and one of the yolks. Meanwhile, finely dice the shallot. Chop the cornichons and capers. Chop the parsley.

Mix the egg and egg yolk, shallot, cornichons, capers and mustard in a bowl with the mayonnaise, a pinch of salt and the cayenne pepper. Just before serving, stir the parsley into the sauce.

Borlotti Beans

PREP 5 MINS / COOK 30–40 MINS

Plump and creamy, borlotti beans are gorgeous in salads and soups, in pasta dishes and casseroles or as an accompaniment to a nicely grilled tuna steak.

SERVES 4

600–700g fresh borlotti beans
4 pinches of sea salt flakes
1 thyme sprig
1 bay leaf
2–3 tablespoons extra-virgin olive oil (optional)
¼ lemon (optional)

TO PREPARE Remove the beans from their pods.

Place the beans in a saucepan, cover with cold water, season with the salt and add the thyme sprig and bay leaf.

Over a medium–high heat, bring to the boil and then reduce to a simmer and continue to cook like this for 30–40 minutes. Taste to check the beans are perfectly soft and just right for you. Drain in a colander. Taste and season accordingly.

They are now ready to eat. If you wish, and while the beans are still hot, stir in the extra-virgin olive oil and a squeeze or two of lemon juice – tasting as you go.

TIPS ABOUT BEANS

- When cooking the beans, you can also add a clove of garlic or sprig of rosemary as this will impart plenty of flavour during the cooking.

- You could allow the beans to cool in their cooking liquor so all the flavours are infused.

- Season the beans while they are still warm, so they absorb the flavours.

Lentils

Follow the cooking instructions on the packet and meanwhile, here are some tips …

TIPS ABOUT LENTILS

- Adding a slice of lemon at the start of cooking gives a delicious acidity to the lentils.

- When cooking lentils, bring them to a gentle simmer and then slightly reduce the heat so they cook as gently as possible. If lentils are cooked too quickly, the water tends to evaporate rather than be absorbed, and they may end up mushy and dry. So it's gently, gently does it.

- Dried lentils can be used when blind baking pastry cases. Save them to use again and again for blind baking.

Cooking Oils

Push your trolley through a supermarket, and soon you will reach the aisle crammed with oils. Oh my God, the choice can be frightening and overwhelming. So I would like to share some thoughts on the subject, and Natalia has kindly helped with nutritional advice.

THOUGHTS ABOUT COOKING OILS

• There are oils that are best for dressing, and then those that are ideal for shallow-frying or deep-frying. For a French dressing or salad dressing, I use a neutral oil, which is unscented, such as sunflower or vegetable. For this type of dressing, avoid an oil that will overpower the flavours of the salad. For instance, coconut oil is just what you want when cooking a Thai or Asian dish but, in a dressing, it will take over the flavours. Equally, avocado oil is perfect when frying, and if you rub it into your skin it will bring eternal youth. In a French dressing, however, it is too rich.

• Then there are those times when you do want the oil to bring its flavour to a dressing. In this case, it would have to be extra-virgin olive oil. All that it needs is a dash of balsamic vinegar or red or white wine vinegar with a pinch of salt and a few turns of pepper, and off you go – you've got your dressing. The finest extra-virgin olive oils are fruity and thin (never heavy) on the palate and, in my opinion, they come from Italy, though there are some excellent ones produced in Provence. Oils are prone to oxidising, so to retain flavours and nutrients, try to keep them in the darkness of a cupboard. I do not cook extra-virgin olive oil at a high temperature.

• The smoking point is the temperature at which an oil starts to burn and smoke. Some oils perform well at high temperatures, which makes them ideal for frying. The more refined an oil, the higher its smoking point. This is because when an oil is refined its impurities and free fatty acids are removed (they can make the oil smoke). Usually, refined oils have a neutral taste and smell, and a clear appearance.

• Unrefined oils, such as extra-virgin olive, tend to be cold-pressed oils (the oil is extracted by pressure, rather than heat). This process helps to retain most of the natural nutrients, which will be destroyed when the oil is overheated. For example, refined olive oil has a smoking point of 199–243°C (390–469°F), while extra-virgin olive oil has a smoking point of 190°C (374°C). Even so, the smoking point of extra-virgin olive oil makes it suitable for many types of cooking, though you do need to learn to control the temperature.

• Other oils with high smoke points include avocado (refined), almond, corn, canola, grapeseed, peanut, safflower, sesame and sunflower. These oils are better suited for cooking at higher temperatures.

• The oils from nuts are healthy and fabulous but often forgotten. My favourite is walnut oil. Just a drizzle or two can add so much, and you will see I have used it in dishes such as the Chicory and Orange Salad (see page 97) and Celeriac Remoulade (see page 111).

Shortcrust Pastry Case

PREP 10 MINS / COOK 30 MINS / CHILL 1½ HOURS

This pastry may be used for both savoury and sweet dishes (such as the Strawberry and Mascarpone Tart on page 263). Cooking the pastry to a golden colour develops a rich, nutty flavour. Meanwhile, the pastry's thickness should be light and delicate, so that the focus is on the filling.

MAKES ABOUT 20CM PASTRY CASE

250g plain flour, plus extra for dusting

2 teaspoons caster sugar

125g unsalted butter, at room temperature and diced, plus extra for greasing the tin

pinch of sea salt

1 medium egg (preferably organic or free-range)

Put the flour, sugar, butter and salt in a large bowl. Using your fingertips, rub the mixture until it has a sandy texture. Create a well in the centre, beat the egg and pour it into the well. Now work the flour and butter mixture into the egg, and then press together to form a ball.

On a lightly floured work surface or board knead the dough with the palms of your hands for 30 seconds maximum – if it is overworked it hardens and loses its crumbling texture. Kneading the dough helps to develop the flour's gluten, which makes dough elastic.

Wrap the pastry in non-pvc clingfilm and refrigerate for 30 minutes.

On a floured board, roll the pastry out to a thickness of about 2mm. Line a greased tart ring with the pastry.

Place the ring on a baking tray lined with greaseproof paper and transfer it to the fridge for 1 hour (to relax the pastry and prevent shrinkage during cooking). The pastry case is now ready for baking.

When it is time to cook the pastry case, preheat the oven to 180°C/160°C fan/gas 4. If blind baking, line the pastry case with greaseproof paper and then add baking beans. Bake for 25–30 minutes until the pastry is lightly golden. Leave it to cool to room temperature before adding the filling.

Armagnac Butter

PREP 3 MINS

A butter to give your Christmas Pudding (see page 238) that extra touch of class and luxury. Cognac may be used instead of Armagnac.

MAKES ABOUT 250G

150g unsalted butter
75g icing sugar
4–8 tablespoons
  Armagnac

With a whisk, cream the butter until white. Beat in the sugar little by little. Add the Armagnac, again little by little, beating the mixture well. If it looks like it might curdle, don't add any more Armagnac (any extra can be poured over the top of the pudding when serving). The butter should be white and foamy. Cover and refrigerate until needed and, for your efforts, allow yourself one small glass of Armagnac.

Vanilla Bean Purée

PREP 3 MINS / COOK 2 MINS

Why waste vanilla bean pods? Vanilla bean paste is widely available in the shops, but if you have leftover pods, this is the way to make the best of them. It will spare them from the bin and save you money. The purée can be stored in a clean jar and kept in the fridge for several weeks.

MAKES 200G

6 vanilla pods
100g caster sugar
100ml recently boiled
  water

TO PREPARE Cut the little stalk off each vanilla pod where it hangs from the tree. Coarsely chop the pods.

Bring the sugar and water to the boil to make a syrup, and then leave to cool to room temperature.

Add the chopped vanilla pods and blend in a liquidiser or food processor on a high speed for about a minute.

Store in a sealed jar to use when a recipe calls for vanilla. A teaspoon is equal to about half a vanilla pod.

'One day I'll hang that sign on
Le Manoir's gates: "Gone fishing".
But not yet! So before then,
let's have a cocktail …'

FAREWELL

Rose Petal Martini

Behind this little recipe there is a huge story. It begins in 2009, when I was presenting the third series of *The Restaurant*. The contestants competed in a variety of challenges, with a grand prize for the winning pair: they'd get to open a restaurant with me. When they started to show off their skills I was horrified, and I still shudder at the memory of one of them trying to cut open a coconut with a small knife. However, I was drawn to the passion, ambition and drive of two young men, JJ, a mixologist, and his fellow contestant, James. They weren't the best cooks, but they could certainly make cocktails. By the end of the series, I chose them as my business partners – but to open a cocktail bar instead of a restaurant. We named it the London Cocktail Club. The place was a real success, thanks mostly to JJ and James's gift, and the team supporting them. We opened another, and then another. We are lucky to have Sarah Willingham, a fellow judge on *The Restaurant*, and a businesswoman with a huge heart. Whenever I'm at the London Cocktail Club, I love a rose petal martini, which was created by JJ and Lee Ottery. Boys might resist it, but the girls can't. Quite dainty, pink and served with a rose petal floating on its surface, it is not, admittedly, the martini that James Bond drinks. But do you know what – it's fun to have cocktails at home, and this one is a cheerful start to many great parties.

MAKES 2 MARTINIS

80ml gin
80ml cranberry juice
30ml rose water
40ml lemon juice
2 red rose petals,
  to garnish

For the sugar syrup
100g caster sugar
100ml water

First, make the sugar syrup. Place the sugar and water in a small saucepan. Leave the sugar to dissolve in the water off the heat for 10 minutes. Now bring to the boil, and leave the syrup to cool down. This will make more syrup than is required for these two cocktails, but the syrup that you don't use can be stored in the fridge ... or you might have to make more cocktails.

Pour all the ingredients into a cocktail shaker with 40ml of the sugar syrup. Add a large handful of ice and shake well for about 20 seconds. The ice accentuates the flavours.

Strain into a pair of chilled martini glasses. To add the essential drama, lay a red rose petal on top of each martini. *Et voilà!*

Index

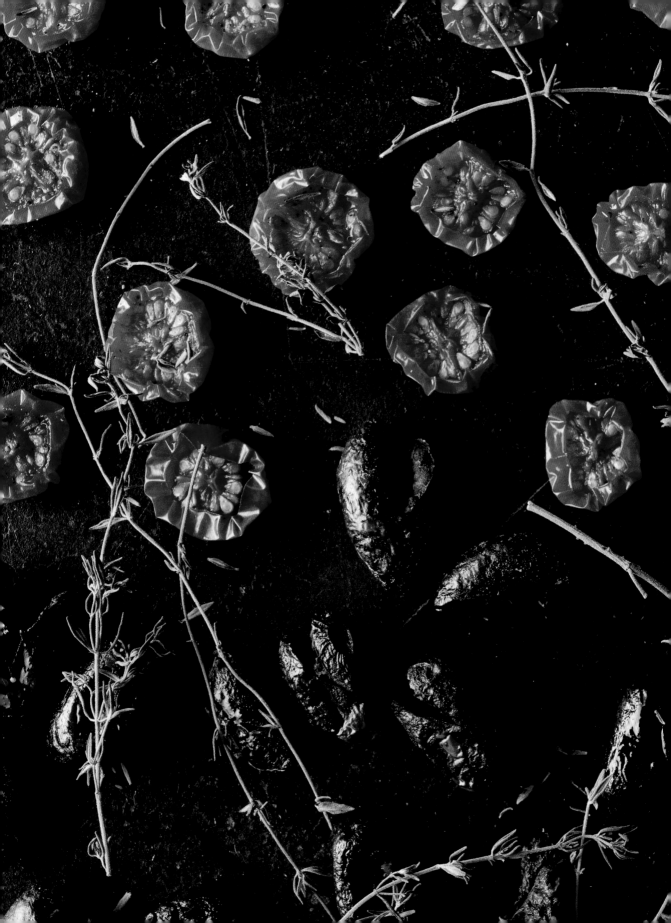

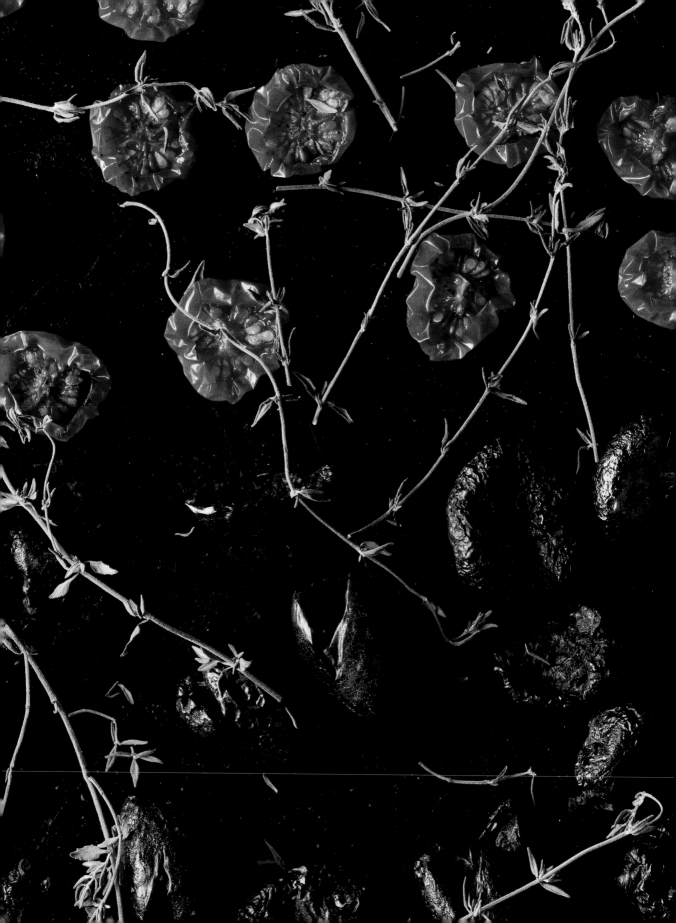

Conversion Charts

Conversions are approximate and have been rounded up or down. Follow one set of measurements only – do not mix metric and imperial.

WEIGHT CONVERSIONS

METRIC	IMPERIAL
10g	¼oz
15g	½oz
20g	¾oz
25g/30g	1oz
35g	1¼oz
40g	1½oz
50g	1¾oz
55g	2oz
60g	2¼oz
70g	2½oz
75g/80g	2¾oz
85g	3oz
100g	3½oz
110g	3¾oz
115g	4oz
120g	4¼oz
125g	4½oz
140g	5oz
150g	5½oz
160g	5¾oz
170g/175g	6oz
180g	6¼oz
200g	7oz
225g	8oz
250g	9oz
280g/285g	10oz
300g	10½oz
320g	11¼oz
325g	11½oz
340g	11¾oz
350g	12oz
375g	13oz
390g	13½oz
400g	14oz
425g	15oz
450g	1lb
500g	1lb 2oz
600g	1lb 5oz
750g	1lb 10oz
900g	2lb
1kg	2lb 4oz
1.3kg	3lb
1.5kg	3lb 5oz
1.6kg	3lb 8oz
2kg	4lb 8oz
2.7kg	6lb

VOLUME CONVERSIONS (LIQUIDS)

METRIC	IMPERIAL	IMPERIAL/CUPS
5ml	1 teaspoon	
15ml	1 tablespoon	
30ml	1fl oz	2 tablespoons
45ml	3 tablespoons	
50ml	2fl oz	
60ml	4 tablespoons	¼ cup
75ml	2½fl oz	⅓ cup
90ml	6 tablespoons	
100ml	3½fl oz	
120ml/125ml	4fl oz	½ cup
150ml	5fl oz (¼ pint)	⅔ cup
175ml	6fl oz	¾ cup
200ml	7fl oz	
225ml	8fl oz	1 cup
250ml	9fl oz	
300ml	10fl oz (½ pint)	
350ml	12fl oz	1½ cups
400ml	14fl oz	
425ml	15fl oz (¾ pint)	
500ml	18fl oz	2 cups
600ml	20fl oz (1 pint)	
700ml	1¼ pints	
900ml	1½ pints	
1 litre	1¾ pints	4 cups
1.2 litres	2 pints	
1.7 litres	3 pints	

VOLUME CONVERSIONS (DRY INGREDIENTS – AN APPROXIMATE GUIDE)

Flour	125g	1 cup
Sugar	200g	1 cup
Butter	225g	1 cup (2 sticks)
Breadcrumbs (dried)	125g	1 cup
Nuts	125g	1 cup
Seeds	160g	1 cup
Dried fruit	150g	1 cup
Dried pulses (large)	175g	1 cup
Grains and small pulses	200g	1 cup

LENGTH

METRIC	IMPERIAL
5mm/½cm	¼ inch
1cm	½ inch
2cm	¾ inch
2.5cm	1 inch
3cm	1¼ inches
4cm	1½ inches
5cm	2 inches
5.5cm	2¼ inches
6cm	2½ inches
7cm	2¾ inches
7.5cm	3 inches
8cm	3¼ inches
9cm	3½ inches
10cm	4 inches
11cm	4¼ inches
12cm	4½ inches
13cm	5 inches
15cm	6 inches
18cm	7 inches
20cm	8 inches
23cm	9 inches
24cm	9½ inches
25cm	10 inches
26cm	10½ inches
27cm	10¾ inches
28cm	11 inches
30cm	12 inches
31cm	12½ inches
33cm	13 inches
34cm	13½ inches
35cm	14 inches
36cm	14¼ inches
38cm	15 inches
40cm	16 inches
41cm	16¼ inches
43cm	17 inches
44cm	17½ inches
46cm	18 inches

OVEN TEMPERATURES

°C	°C WITH FAN	°F	GAS MARK
110°C	90°C	225°F	¼
120°C	100°C	250°F	½
140°C	120°C	275°F	1
150°C	130°C	300°F	2
160°C	140°C	325°F	3
170°C	150°C	340°F	3½
180°C	160°C	350°F	4
190°C	170°C	375°F	5
200°C	180°C	400°F	6
220°C	200°C	425°F	7
230°C	210°C	450°F	8
240°C	220°C	475°F	9

Acknowledgements

The feast has finished. Having shared food and laughter, it is now time for farewells and a moment to say thank you from the heart. When it comes to a good meal, appreciation is as essential as appetite.

There was a ritual in my childhood that I have never forgotten. We would all be at the table and ready to eat, and then, with the tip of a bread knife, my father would make the sign of the cross on the top of the loaf. Only once the bread was crossed could we lift our knives and forks or soup spoons. Our father's custom was a silent acknowledgement for what we were about to enjoy. Although I must tell you that he was not giving thanks to God – my father, you see, was an atheist. 'It is a mark of respect,' he told me. 'We must acknowledge the hard work that has gone into the creation of what reaches our table.'

Of course, every cook relishes a bit of praise. We know, however, that we could never have the compliments without the help of others, such as the farmers and fishermen, butchers and fishmongers, and the producers of beautiful wines and extraordinary cheeses. A book, like a meal, is not the work of one. *Simply Raymond* is, in fact, not simply me. Many others have smoothed the path, from concept to manuscript, and then to publication, the launch of the book and the hope that you will cook from it.

Therefore I am extremely pleased to be able to applaud those who have contributed to this particular feast. The words that follow are a mark of respect, the cross upon the crust …

I would like to begin with praise for that great man, Adam Johnson, my Head Development Chef. Adam is a protégé who has been with me for many years. Throughout that time, and during this project, his assistance and support have been fundamental, vital. Adam, I am so truly grateful to you. Also, I owe a huge thank you to Daniel Fitzhugh, Assistant Development Chef.

Lindsey Evans and Kate Miles have been the most welcoming and warm-hearted of hosts. At Headline Home, Lindsey and Kate and their team have indeed made me feel very much at home. I have been encouraged and spurred on by their passion for this project, and by their enthusiasm and wise advice.

What a great pleasure it has been to work once again with Chris Terry, the highly talented photographer who took the stunning pictures. Emma Lahaye is a superb props stylist, and a joy. I am honoured, as well, to have worked with Nathan Burton, the designer who has so cleverly united the words with the photographs. As the skilful copy editor, Kay Halsey has played a significant role, and I appreciate her considerate input. My thanks to Vicky Orchard, Amber Burlinson and Jill Cole, who read and corrected proofs, sparing a blush or two. Or even three.

Now I shall raise my glass four times, to toast each of the following people at Headline: Louise Rothwell in Production; Jessica Farrugia in Publicity and Lucie Sharpe and Vicky Abbott in Marketing. I'm raising my glass once more, this time to toast Rebecca Bader in Sales. Oh, I feel a bit tipsy.

I am so grateful to Lydia Shevell, my business director. I owe a sincere debt of gratitude to my personal assistants, Leanda Pearman and Megan Bint. A big thanks to my literary agent, Charlie Brotherstone.

In the making of this book, the team at Le Manoir aux Quat'Saisons have been helpful and enthusiastic, and I pay special thanks to Eveline Noort (General Manager), Niall Kingston (Hotel Manager), Gary Jones (Executive Head Chef) and Chef Pâtissier, Benoit Blin, who shared some sweet, delicious recipes in the Desserts section. My thanks, as well, to Mark Peregrine, Director of the Raymond Blanc Cookery School, and his team, who constantly show our eager students how to cook beautiful, simple food at home. I am always grateful to Anne-Marie Owens, who oversees the twelve magnificent gardens at Le Manoir. And a massive thank you to my wonderful friends at Belmond, who have been supportive throughout.

At Brasserie Blanc, my thanks are due to Clive Fretwell, who oversees the kitchens (and in the early days of Le Manoir was head chef) and to Shailesh Kumar Jha, who very kindly shared his recipes for vegetable kadai and boiled rice. My thanks to our world-class suppliers, especially Aubrey Allen (which, from the very beginning, has delivered to Le Manoir and Brasserie Blanc) and to Rhug Estate in North Wales, and Johnny Godden from Flying Fish.

A big hug for my sons, Olivier and Sebastien, who are a constant source of support and friendship. Their nickname for Maman Blanc was 'Mother Theresa on speed'. They love to cook and they tried a few recipes from the book, including their favourite salade of saucisse de Morteau.

Words cannot express all my love and gratitude to Natalia, my companion of 18 years, for her patience and overwhelming kindness. Her enthusiasm for life has always brightened mine. As a nutritionist, Natalia has made a valuable contribution to this book and shown, once again, that good ingredients and nutrition make wholesome and delicious food.

Also, thank you to Tata, who is wonderful and has helped me so often, and sorted out my English grammar headaches as if they are never headaches for her.

As for James Steen, the brilliant writer and friend with whom I have worked for many years, thank you with all my heart. James, put down that cup of tea – it's time to share an exquisite bottle of Gevrey-Chambertin. We deserve it.

Here I am with Adam Johnson, when life was a bowl of cherries.

Photography © Chris Terry 2020

Photograph on p.15 (bottom, left) © Paul Wilkinson Photography Ltd
Photographs on p.4, 12 and 15 (excluding bottom, left) from the author's collection
Photograph on p.315 © Adam Johnson

First published in Great Britain in 2021
by Headline Home
an imprint of Headline Publishing Group

1

Cataloguing in Publication Data is available from the British Library

Backdrop on p.8 and 16 by canvasbackdrops.co.uk

ISBN 978 1 4722 6760 3
eBook ISBN 978 1 4722 6761 0

Commissioning Editor: Lindsey Evans
Senior Editor: Kate Miles
Design: Nathan Burton
Photography: Chris Terry
Food Stylist: Adam Johnson
Home Economist Assistant: Daniel Fitzhugh
Prop Stylist: Emma Lahaye
Prop Stylist Assistant: Max Robinson
Copy Editor: Kay Halsey
Proofreaders: Vicky Orchard, Amber Burlinson and Jill Cole
Indexer: Caroline Wilding

Printed and Bound in Italy by LEGO S.p.A.
Colour reproduction by Alta Image

HEADLINE PUBLISHING GROUP

An Hachette UK Company
Carmelite House
50 Victoria Embankment
London EC4Y 0DZ

www.headline.co.uk
www.hachette.co.uk